In over twenty-five years of pastoral ministry I have collected a few 'go-to' books. These are resources that I would recommend to people whether they are leaning into theology, discipleship or apologetics, or facing catastrophic loss and distress. As a writer, Ruth will draw you in with the raw and real, as a teacher she will delve into solid theology regarding divorce and remarriage, and as a daughter your heart will break with hers. Then she will build a bridge of recovery, both spiritual and practical, to set a foundation of hope for the future. Having had the honor of being Ruth's pastor over the last several years, I can attest to her character and the work of grace in her life. (Un)Faithful is now on my list of 'go-to' references, and should be in the library of every leader who works with people.

Jeff Ecklund
Author of "Wholehearted"
Lead Pastor, House of the Lord
Oldtown, Idaho

(Un)Faithful is the most comprehensive book I have ever read on recovery from adultery and betrayal. Each chapter navigates the reader through the reality of pain, grief and healing. The theological soundness of Ruth's scripture use is impressive, allowing the reader to come to their own conclusion with grace and faith about their personal path forward.

Fire sister, this is for you. Hope and healing is just ahead. I am so thankful for Ruth, and her passion to dig deep, finding the hidden waters of restoration.

Raydeane Owens
Author of "Heaven-Earth" and "Brave One"
Co-Lead Pastor, Heart of the City Church
Coeur d'Alene, Idaho

From the moment I met Ruth, I knew this book was imperative to helping many women heal. As a pastor, I often refer broken women who are the victims of affairs and betrayal to certain books or counselors. I was relieved to find another resource I can recommend to women to help them walk out their healing, but I literally had no idea how much this book would wreck me. I thought I understood pain, but when I read these pages, I empathized with the pain of betrayal and have even greater compassion for anyone going through this heartbreaking journey.

Written as if straight from God's heart, you will see God's hand at work and will feel His compassion as He walks you through your healing journey. Ruth's powerful word imagery is like oil on a canvas, her poetry is so heartfelt, and I love how each chapter concludes with thought-provoking questions and space for personal reflection. I highly recommend (Un)Faithful to anyone who has faced betrayal, and if you are a pastor, counselor, or your vocation is to walk women through a healing process, this will be an especially beneficial tool for you.

Kari Jennings
Pastor, Breakthrough Church
Yakima, Washington

There is healing in each page of Ruth's story. Every aspect of recovery is addressed, and women who have walked through the trauma of an affair will find rich empathy and a sense of purpose here. One easily senses the voice of the Holy Spirit through the words in this book as Ruth speaks truth, clarity, and hope. It is my prayer that this work of written art gets into the hands of every woman whose life was shattered by an affair so that it can be an aid in the crucial healing that is desperately needed.

April Ashburn
Executive Pastor, Higher Vision Church
Valencia, California

This is a book that we all wish didn't have to be written. The hope is that every man would be faithful to every wife and that no one would experience the wounds caused by adultery. The reality is that sin and evil spiritual forces are at work in this world, so there are countless women who desperately need the comfort and counsel found in this book. As I read through the pages, I was moved not only by Ruth's evident compassion for every victim, but also the authority with which she brings biblical insights about matters of covenant, marriage, forgiveness, grief, and identity.

This book is like a trail guide through the dark forest of marital unfaithfulness, but because there is such a strong testimony of the restoring power of Christ, I believe every reader will gain hope that there is a way out of that deep darkness into light once again.

Bonnie Pue
Author of "Weight of Wings" and "Making a Clean Break"
Co-founder of The Union Movement
Mission, BC, Canada

In (Un)Faithful, we are moved by Ruth Erickson's story, her journey, and her healing through scripture and faith. A must-read for anyone facing an affair.

Matthias Barker, LMHC
Psychotherapist & Content Creator
Nashville, Tennessee

The book you are holding in your hand is an absolute gift! As someone who has walked a similar path, you will be hard-pressed to find a more powerful and anointed testimony of God's incredible love and grace than what's written in the pages of this book. Ruth's writing is compelling and honest as she unpacks details of her broken past and the ways in which God intervened. Within the pages of (Un)Faithful are hidden treasures visible to those eager to find truth. Crafted within each chapter are tools to help rebuild and create something so beautiful out of what was once broken and discarded.

The truth of God's word so skillfully woven into Ruth's own redemptive story is a scalpel in the hand of the Master surgeon, extracting the poisoned and damaged areas of the soul with extreme precision and care.

There is hope! You have a future! Ruth says it best herself when she writes, "Healing is not found in a formula or in specific steps, but rather, in a Person, in the God who made me and sustains me." I pray that you will be changed by God's unfailing love as you read Ruth's story.

Marty Meyer
Speaker, Pastoral Coach and Mentor
Women's Ministry Director, Hope Church
Kalispell, Montana

(Un)Faithful is the book I looked for and couldn't find in my years of pastoring. With wisdom and vulnerability, Ruth shares her story of healing after a spouse has been unfaithful, continually pointing the reader to the greater story of God's faithfulness. Weaving together poetry, personal testimony, and sound Biblical teaching, she brings a grace-filled message of hope for all who find themselves walking this painful path. Her 'fire sisters' will find in these pages a sage guide and an invitation to deeper wholeness from the One who will never break His covenant of love with them. I am grateful for Ruth's willingness to bare her heart, and expectant for how her words will bless and rebuild shattered lives.

Aimée Walker
Author of "But I Flourish" and "Prayers for a Generation"
Co-founder of The Devoted Collective
Auckland, New Zealand

A redemptive and healing guide for those journeying through the unfaithfulness of a partner. I love Ruth and her heart to gift her story to others navigating the unthinkable. As a pastor who works with women in situations like this, I will recommend this read. Thank you, Ruth, for writing with a beautiful blend of the real yet redeemed!

Jerushah Tanner
Executive Pastor at Living Hope
Beaverton, Oregon

(UN) FAITHFUL

Torn Curtain Publishing
Wellington, New Zealand
www.torncurtainpublishing.com

© Copyright 2022 Ruth Erickson. All rights reserved.

ISBN Softcover 978-0-6453977-3-4
ISBN EPub 978-0-6453977-4-1

No portion of this book may be reproduced, stored in a retrieval system or transmitted in any form or by any means—electronic, mechanical, photocopy, recording or otherwise—except for brief quotations in printed reviews or promotion, without prior written permission from the author.

Unless otherwise noted, all scripture is taken from the Holy Bible, New Living Translation, copyright © 1996, 2004, 2015 by Tyndale House Foundation. Used by permission of Tyndale House Publishers, Inc., Carol Stream, Illinois 60188. All rights reserved.

Scripture quotations marked ESV are from the ESV® Bible (The Holy Bible, English Standard Version®), copyright © 2001 by Crossway, a publishing ministry of Good News Publishers. Used by permission. All rights reserved.

Scripture quotations marked NASB are taken from the New American Standard Bible®, Copyright © 1960, 1971, 1977, 1995, 2020 by The Lockman Foundation. Used by permission. All rights reserved. www.lockman.org

Scripture quotations marked NIV are taken from the Holy Bible, New International Version®, NIV®. Copyright © 1973, 1978, 1984, 2011 by Biblica, Inc.™ Used by permission of Zondervan. All rights reserved worldwide.

Scripture quotations marked MSG are taken from THE MESSAGE, copyright © 1993, 2002, 2018 by Eugene H. Peterson. Used by permission of NavPress. All rights reserved. Represented by Tyndale House Publishers, a Division of Tyndale House Ministries.

Scripture quotations marked YLT are from the 1898 YOUNG'S LITERAL TRANSLATION OF THE HOLY BIBLE by J.N. Young, (Author of the Young's Analytical Concordance), public domain.

Cover design by Sarah Mejia @covestudiodesign

Cataloguing in Publishing Data
  Title: (Un)Faithful: Finding Healing After Your Husband's Affair
  Author: Ruth Erickson
  Subjects: Christian Living, Family & Relationships, Women's Interests, Adultery & Divorce

(UN) FAITHFUL

Finding Healing After Your Husband's Affair
(Whether Your Marriage Survives Or Not)

RUTH ERICKSON

CONTENTS

Preface: My Marriage

Introduction

Prose: I Will Never Forget

1.	Marriage: The Real Thing	15
2.	Adultery: God's Perspective	31
3.	Suffering: Nearness to God	49
4.	Trauma: Getting to Safety	65
5.	Identity: Rediscovering Who You Are	81
6.	Lies: Fighting Back with Truth	97
7.	Reframing: Making Sense of Your Story	115
8.	Decisions: Moving Forward with Wisdom	125
9.	Divorce: Saying a Gracious Goodbye	142
10.	Forgiveness: Finding Freedom in Release	163
11.	Grief: Being Present in the Process	182
12.	Healing: Being Held by Jesus	201

Epilogue

Appendix

Recommended Resources

Acknowledgments

The dam breaks
Pain so gaping and hollow
It is beyond tears
Swallows me whole
Crushes my chest
My world is gone
Where can I keep living?

This new place is fresh
Exhausting
Haunted

There is light, but it is torment
Memories are a flood
Love is a noose
Pain is food and drink and breath

My heart beats, but how?
It is gone
He took it and lost it along the way

Maybe it is buried with his

Silence, cold sheets, empty coffee mugs
My constant companions
Mocking my attempts at repair

No.
I've been replaced and erased and trampled
Stop trying to feel okay
You're not okay
You are dying and it is slow

God … who made me and carries me and weeps alongside
I don't understand

The rain falls on us all
But why does it burn
Like acid
Like laughter
At my reckless hope and prayers for
Something More

It may come to pass
But not today

Today is a hole
Full of empty air and broken promises

Breathing
Gasping
Surviving

Barely enough
To know I am still alive

MY MARRIAGE

My marriage was beautiful. In my mind's eye, it was like a seven-year-old child that my husband and I had created together—somewhat imperfect and messy, but indescribably valuable and precious to me. I fed it, protected it, dreamed over it, and ached over it, doing my part to keep it healthy. I wasn't perfect at this. I made mistakes that hurt it from time to time, and I had to apologize. But I gave it my very best, because I loved my husband.

I was so connected to my marriage. When it hurt, I hurt. When it thrived, I thrived. I thought my husband loved it, too. After all, it belonged to him as well. He had promised to protect it, and I truly believed he would.

Slowly, I sensed a shift in my husband. I shrugged it off, thinking it was just a phase he was going through. But he began criticizing our marriage more and more often, and quickly he became cold towards it. Suddenly, to my shock and horror, my husband grabbed a knife and plunged it into the heart of our seven-year-old vows.

Screaming in disbelief, I clutched the bleeding body and held it close to me. In terror, I looked to my husband to help, to save it. *Why did he do this? Was it an accident?* His face was numb, unresponsive. As I pleaded with him, he told me it was my fault, and stabbed again. My screams roared out of me; I was unhinged. He told me to be quiet, that my screaming was hurting his ears, that I was always overreacting. Then he walked away.

I frantically tried to stop the bleeding, to breathe life back into the limp, beloved body of my marriage. Wailing, I rocked it back and forth, begging it not to die. It did not respond. It did not move, did not breathe. I was devastated; it was dead.

I had heard of other marriages being killed like this, but never thought it could happen to mine—we loved each other too much for that to be our ending. Remembering stories of resurrections, I begged my husband to return to the scene, to call on heaven to bring life back from death. I waited, praying, hoping, that the murder would be undone. That this child could live again.

My husband told me he would come. He took a few steps toward us and my heart flickered with hope. Then he turned and walked away into the darkness. I waited with the body, every second a horror.

After three months of waiting, still covered in blood and tears, the Lord whispered to my heart, *It is time to bury the dead body.*

With shaking hands, I started digging. With a tear-stained face, I buried the treasure of my life. With deep grief, I signed my name on the death certificate, the divorce decree. This horrifying paper was an acknowledgment of the loss of a life I longed to grow old with. A murder I did not commit.

INTRODUCTION

Welcome, friends. My desire in writing this book is to connect to the shattered hearts of women who have been violated by an affair and to breathe comfort, hope, and courage into their lives. If that is you, sister, this book is yours. We have walked through fire, you and I, and our hearts are connected. Every word on the page, every tear I've cried, every step of healing I've taken, every scar I have from walking through my own fire, was for you. We are Fire Sisters, and even if we have not met, I love you. You are the reason for this book.

Whether the fire of the affair is still raging and there are big decisions ahead, or you are years past the affair and desire deeper healing, I am honored to journey with you, and offer you whatever companionship, wisdom, and hope I have.

I need to be upfront about the fact that I believe adultery murders a marriage. I also need to be upfront that I believe that God can resurrect dead things. I believe both, which means that I fully support women who acknowledge the death of their marriage through divorce, as well as women who contend for the resurrection power of a restored marriage. If you are committed to waiting, or you have renewed your marriage, I am for you. I trust you; I believe in you. If you have decided that divorce is your way forward after the affair, I am for you. I trust you; I believe in you. If you are still in that waiting place and do not know the future of your marriage, I am for you. I trust you; I believe in you.

My testimony is one of burying a dead marriage and finding healing and restoration in and after divorce. It is the only story I can tell because it is the only story I have lived. If you've reconciled with your husband, there may be parts of this book that feel like they don't apply to you. That is okay. Glean what you can, and know that I am cheering you on as the Lord leads you.

I know there may be many who read this who have not been violated by an affair. All are welcome here. Please understand that the language and tone of this book are crafted specifically with my Fire Sisters in mind. They deserve my special attention and the ministry of my story. You may, however, find woven into these pages some healing and hope for your own broken places. Deep calls to deep.

Perhaps you are the loved one of a Fire Sister, seeking understanding and wisdom on how to support her. Thank you for investing your time into her. As you learn all she must unravel and endure, cover her with your love. Trust that the Lord will guide her through, and know that she needs support and connection more than advice. Believe me, your presence is healing, even when you don't have answers.

You may be a leader wanting to better understand those you guide and shepherd. Thank you for bringing a teachable heart and for investing the time that is needed to care for the women (and men) you encounter who are devastated by infidelity. Your voice carries weight, and it is crucial that you have a biblical foundation and the compassion of Christ as you lead.

You may be a man whose wife has had an affair. While I am writing to the female heart and using language directed towards women, many shadows of your story will be found in these pages. My brother, you are not alone. Although your pain as a man is unique, I pray you find some comfort here.

You may even have been the perpetrator of an affair and are hoping to find your way back to the heart you have broken. You will not find judgement here. Bless you for the courage and humility to look this pain in the face. There can be no true reconciliation without acknowledgement and responsibility, but repentance and restoration are more than possible through surrender to Jesus. I hope this book deepens your understanding and leads you to new levels of love, sacrifice, and wholeness.

JESUS AT THE CENTER

My whole life, including the death of my marriage, can only be fully known and understood in the context of my faith in Jesus. His covering and presence are on every page. I know there may be readers who do not know or trust Him as I do. Again, all are welcome here. Read on. Just know that *He* is my story. He is the answer to all my impossible questions, the healer of my deepest agonies. It was He who held me through the darkest nights and walked with me through this fierce fire. He will be referenced at every turn, because any wisdom and hope I have to offer are found in Him.

I am confident that God led me through my fire in a profound and supernatural way. He was, and is, a rock and a shelter to me. I believe that every step was guarded and purposeful, that He led me in the way I should go. However, it's incredibly important to me that I am clear that my healing was not found in a formula or in specific steps, but rather, in a Person, in the God who made me and sustains me. I'm not here to tell you a ten-step program to get you back on your feet. It's never that simple. But I believe with all my heart that God has answers and comfort for you, and my hope is not to tell you which decisions to make, but to provide some signposts to help you see in which direction to head. Head toward home—that place where truth and security find roots deep inside of you, where you connect with your Creator and see the true image of His heart in yours. God's Word is your map and the compass you need to lead you there.

The most helpful relationships during the death of my marriage were those who did not tell me what they thought I should do, but pointed me to Jesus and trusted me to hear His voice. Sister, I trust you to hear His voice. You may not know how, or believe that you can, but I know deep in my spirit that He is faithful to hear your cries and to speak to you at the right moments. It is my prayer that He speaks through me, not to tell you *what* decisions to make, but *Who* to seek. God will guide you to decisions that you can be confident in, and proud of. Whether your marriage survives and is renewed, or whether you walk through divorce, my hope is that you heal well and find yourself whole-hearted.

TRUTH WITH HONOR

It is my desire to tell you the real story, the whole story, because God is in the details. But, as I tell everyone with whom I share my experience, it does not belong solely to me. There are others inside this story, and all the hurt and wrong that has been done to me is forgiven. That means I do not give anyone permission to take offense on my behalf. Everyone represented in these pages is loved by Jesus, and I want to honor them. They have their own story to tell. All the judgment for their sin, and mine, has been borne on Jesus' shoulders, and He is the only One worthy to judge it. Names and identifying details have been left out because I want to honor the privacy and dignity of those whose lives are entangled with mine.

I am committed to the truth, and not just my version of it, which surely is incomplete. My perspective is limited, and just like every relational story, there are two sides. Surely there have been things over the years that I have misunderstood, even misremembered. However, I trust that God's perspective is complete and trustworthy. The truths in these pages do not originate with me; the truth I ultimately desire that you anchor to, is what we find together in Jesus and His Word. Jesus says in John 8:31-32, "If you continue in My word, then you are truly My disciples; and you will know the truth, *and the truth will set you free*" (NASB).

INTRODUCTION

I want you to be set free, sister. So, I will tell the truth, and I will tell it in love in the hope that you will find keys to unlock healing and that it will point you to where your ultimate healing lies: in the story and the truth found in Jesus.

THE SISTERHOOD

This is a sisterhood that no one ever desires to be part of. The initiation is involuntary and brutal, and no woman in the tribe would ever hope for another sister to be added. The cost is unimaginable, inhumane; the fire of infidelity cruel and unsparing. The women who have walked through this fire regret that anyone else has to join them in it. But here we are, sister. You have been betrayed, violated, lied to, and traumatized. You've been a victim of an ugly and awful affair. I am so sorry. The women who have gone before you would give anything to spare you this pain, but none of us can undo what has been done to you.

There are no words to describe how much I yearn to be able to give you all the answers you long for. What I wouldn't give to offer you a short-cut to healing, a simple, all-in-one solution to this monumental problem you are facing. I'd love nothing more than to tell you there is a fast pass, an alternate route to the other side of the torment. But there is no way around this; only through.

When I look back on my story, I know that no one else could have walked it out for me. I cannot take this cup from you, or make the decisions you may have in front of you. And honestly, only you deserve the honor of owning your life and your story, even this brutal chapter. It belongs to you. So, I cannot give you simple answers to this complex unraveling of your life. What I can do is show you my scars and share with you my hope. While our experiences are unique, there are threads of connection that I pray will testify to your grief so that you feel seen.

If I could, I would make you a cup of tea, curl up on the couch, look into your eyes, and listen. I would cry with you and pray over you and trust that as our lives touch, healing would flow to you. I've had the privilege of walking beside many women in this way. As I've coached women through their healing after an affair, I have been honored to bear witness to the most broken and beautiful souls, just like yours. Yes, *you* are beautiful. Your suffering has not diminished you, sister. You may not see your strength, but I see it. I know it's there, and I will believe in you, even if you don't have what it takes to believe in yourself yet. I wish I could tell you this face to face, but I am grateful for the gift that it is to know you are reading my words now.

As we journey together, I will do my best to be sensitive to your hurting heart, and to be careful with my words. There is so much I do not know about you and your story, and I do not presume to have all the answers. I am in no way a perfect guide, and there may be some things that I share that are not for you. Take the best I have to offer you, and leave the rest.

I will, however, be fighting for you. There is a real darkness at work that has attacked your life. The lies of the enemy have ensnared your husband, and believe me, the enemy has lies he wants to whisper to you too. I will not have it. Not on my watch. I am going to speak truth over you as clearly and fiercely as I can. You deserve to be fought for, and I am up for the task. Some things may be difficult for you to hear or accept. Take my words as one perspective, and always weigh out your big decisions in community with people you trust. There is no substitute for in-person, real life counsel. But just know that I will not be holding back when it comes to speaking life and truth over you, and that my deepest desire is for you to connect to the heart of Jesus, that He might heal you.

Jesus is not some cosmic overlord, sitting back, emotionlessly watching you hurt. No, He is close, weeping with you. He knows what it is to suffer, He knows what it is to be betrayed. Not only was He betrayed, beaten, and murdered by those He came to love, He continues to be rejected, misunderstood, and wrongly accused by

INTRODUCTION

the world. He created us with a free will, because He wants to be chosen. He knows what it feels like for someone to make the wrong choice, to choose another, and He understands your pain. Believe me, He really does get it—God's covenant people have a history of unfaithfulness that has enraged Him and broken His heart. He wants to hold you close and shield you from the lies of the enemy that have set your world on fire. Stay near to Him as we journey. He is the rock, the comfort, and the truth you need, the One who has promised to be with you as you walk through this fire.

I encourage you to take your time with the application questions and the prayer at the end of each chapter—you'll find space there to journal your thoughts. You may have to pace yourself in reading and responding. That's okay. This heart work is hard work and will take courage. But you are so brave, and we can get through this together.

On behalf of the sisterhood, I lend our strength to you. We all bear scars, but many of us have been made whole. There is hope for you yet. You may not be able to hear our voices cheering you on, but I believe your spirit will be lifted by the prayers and love of many women who have gone before you. You are not alone. We are standing with you, and the God who has strengthened and sustained us is with you and will never leave you.

When you go through deep waters, I will be with you.
When you go through rivers of difficulty, you will not drown.
When you walk through the fire of oppression, you will not be burned up;
the flames will not consume you.

Isaiah 43:2

"I WILL NEVER FORGET"

I will never forget the look in his eyes the moment my husband saw me walk down the aisle. All of our romance, passion, and friendship culminated into that moment. His eyes told the story. My heart fluttered, my knees were weak, but walking toward him was the most natural thing. He was my home. I felt radiant, confident, beautiful. All of the preparation for our wedding day, all the fussing with my hair and makeup, all of the adjusting of the dress and the flowers melted away as I looked into his eyes. His love for me lit up the whole room, and I felt like I was living in my sweetest dream.

I will never forget the look in his eyes the moment he knew that I knew about the affair. All of our romance, passion, and friendship shattered in that moment. His eyes told the story. My heart collapsed; my body was on fire. Rage and disbelief and panic surged through me with sharp electricity. My home was gone. I felt small, desperate, pathetic. All of the hard work of marriage, all of the building a life together, all of my hope for our future crumbled as I looked into his eyes. His indifference for me sent chills down my spine, and I felt like I was living in my worst nightmare.

1

MARRIAGE

THE REAL THING

It may seem unexpected to start a book about my fire-walk through adultery and divorce with a chapter about marriage. My marriage failed, right? Well, while my story hinges on the affair, it did not start there. It started with a beautiful, valuable union—a holy covenant—and two people dreaming of the future together. Two people who could never have envisaged the pain that lay ahead.

Marriage is one of the most significant relationships any of us enter—you know more than most how deeply this relationship has impacted you. In every culture, in every time period, marriage has been the soil of the most fruitful and most painful parts of human life. If marriage and fidelity were not important, adultery would not be a problem. Yet the depth of the pain caused by an extra-marital affair is a signal to us of the enormity of the value of marriage, and in order to process this violation of it, we must define the terms and importance of marriage itself. As we try to unpack the tangled mess of adultery, what went terribly wrong, we need to understand what is right. We need a true north, a compass to help us journey well. So, we will start with what is right and true.

When a counterfeit agent is trained to identify fake money, you would assume they would study the counterfeit options— what they look and feel like, the methods used to create a fake. Instead, he or she studies the real thing, extensively researching, experiencing, and memorizing the real deal. As they focus on what is true, what is valid, they can easily discern a forgery.

Adultery is a forgery of love. It is a counterfeit, a fake, and a lie. To study the real thing, we must start with the Author of love: God. God created marriage. God created you, and He designed you to receive, experience, and reflect real, authentic, faithful love inside of marriage.

I know it is painful to think of what your marriage should be when you are experiencing something so far below the love God intended you to know. But it is important to have your feet on something sturdy as you walk through this storm. Your world is shaken, and confusion and chaos threaten to take you under. To find your path forward, you'll need the solid ground of God's design and desire for you.

When the affair was exposed, I remember feeling like I did not know who to trust. I couldn't trust my husband, and I felt like I could barely trust myself. But deep in my spirit, I knew that God was real and good and safe. I knew that His Word is the expression of His heart, and I could trust it. It was understanding what He created me for that eventually enabled me to confidently move forward, and I believe it will do the same for you.

We must not let the perversion of love and marriage define our view. The enemy's strongest weapon is lies, so we will guard ourselves with the truth. Rather than letting our broken experiences of marriage define reality, we will look to God's Word to see the real thing.

THE FIRST MARRIAGE

From Genesis to Revelation, we see marriage created and honored by God. The Bible both begins and ends with a wedding. In the Garden of Eden, God created Adam and Eve to complement, serve, and delight one another. God did not want Adam to be alone, so He decided, "I will make a helper who is just right for him" (Genesis 2:18).

His creation wasn't complete until He created Eve, Adam's counterpart, his helper. Our English word 'helper' can carry connotations that are misleading and incomplete. Using the phrase "the help" conjures up images of a demeaning class-based hierarchy that often draws from a dark history of the subjugation of certain ethnic groups as obligated to serve, with little to no value or agency. This is *not* what the Hebrew writer meant in Genesis. Eve wasn't created as an assistant, a sub-par, low-grade tool for Adam to use to help him get what he wanted. This word, *ezer* in Hebrew, is the same word used for *God Himself* sixty-six times in Scripture. It refers to God's power, protection, help, strength, and ability to rescue. This kind of life-saving, strength-building help, was what God designed for Adam in the person of Eve. The fact that the same word could be used to describe God *and* woman, gives a great deal of honor and worth to her. In this way, she reflects and images her Creator—just as her husband does.

It can also be easy to miss the rich theology in the words used to describe how these humans are made in God's image. In Genesis 1:26, God said, "Let us make man in our image, after our likeness" (ESV). The word 'God' here is plural in Hebrew and provides our first insight into the Trinity—the three-in-one nature of God. The word 'man' in this passage is also plural (understood as mankind). This subtly, but significantly communicates that God exists in plurality *and* unity, and that He designed humans for that as well. Verse 27 confirms this: "So God created man in his own image, in the image of God he created him; male and female he created them." Both Adam and Eve were created in God's image, together, *and* individually. They image God on their own as complete selves, but they also image Him in a unique way when they are together.

Not only does Scripture illustrate God's value for the male and female relationship, but Adam himself echoes the value and worth of the partnership. Before being tainted by sin, Adam illustrates the ideal response of a husband to his wife. In Hebrew literature, Adam's reaction to seeing Eve for the first time was poetry, a song of honor, praise, and adoration over his wife.

> *"At last!" the man exclaimed. "This one is bone from my bone, and flesh from my flesh! She will be called 'woman,' because she was taken from 'man.'"*
>
> Genesis 2:23

Adam affirmed Eve's God-given value and worth as he gratefully received the gift she was to him. Their connection to each other and the intimacy they shared in their relationship depicted the Triune nature of God, and as love flowed back and forth between them, their union reflected glory back to God, whose love and union within the Trinity is perfect.

It was only after God created this pair, united as one flesh, that He deemed His creation "very good," and rested (Genesis 1:31). This union, this joining, is not only blessed by God, but is designed and intended by Him. God's will is for this union to be permanent and unbroken, honored equally by both people.

GOD'S VALUE FOR MARRIAGE

God's Word reveals His value for marriage just as clearly in the New Testament. As Jesus steps onto the stage of history, He affirms the design of marriage, with echoes back to Genesis:

> *But from the beginning of creation, 'God made them male and female.' 'Therefore a man shall leave his father and mother and hold fast to his wife, and the two shall become one flesh.' So they are no longer two but one flesh. What therefore God has joined together, let not man separate.*
>
> Mark 10:6-9 (ESV)

We see that marriage is not only a union between a man and woman, but that God has an active role in joining them together. The separation and tearing of the one flesh are forbidden by Jesus Himself.

The apostle Paul also gives instructions to the early church on marriage, and how husbands and wives are to treat one another. Amazingly, this marriage relationship is used to describe the Church's union with Jesus:

> *For wives, this means submit to your husbands as to the Lord. For a husband is the head of his wife **as Christ is the head of the church**. He is the Savior of his body, the church. **As the church submits to Christ**, so you wives should submit to your husbands in everything.*
>
> *For husbands, this means love your wives, **just as Christ loved the church**. He gave up his life for her to make her holy and clean, washed by the cleansing of God's word. He did this to present her to himself as a glorious church without a spot or wrinkle or any other blemish. Instead, she will be holy and without fault. In the same way, husbands ought to love their wives as they love their own bodies. For a man who loves his wife actually shows love for himself. No one hates his own body but feeds and cares for it, **just as Christ cares for the church**. And we are members of his body.*
>
> *As the Scriptures say, 'A man leaves his father and mother and is joined to his wife, and the two are united into one.' This is a great mystery, but **it is an illustration of the way Christ and the church are one**.*
>
> Ephesians 5:22-32 (emphasis mine)

You can see how often Paul relates human marriage to the union between the Church and Christ. What an incredible honor marriage has, to be used as an illustration of how the Creator and the creation relate to one another. Regardless of whether your lens is egalitarian or complementarian, the Scripture's value for the humanity and dignity of each partner is undeniable, and fidelity is an absolute requirement of biblical marriage.

Based on this letter to the Ephesian church, a woman is to prefer her husband, putting him first and letting him lead as Christ leads the Church. Christ is a high standard for the husband, and God knows it! The man is expected to lay down his life for his wife, serving her, cherishing her, protecting her. This kind of leadership requires that the man prefers his wife. I do not know a woman who does not want to be treated as preferred, protected, and promoted.

Of course, history has shown us that when leadership is perverted and the strength that men have is twisted into control and self-serving domination, abuse is the result. In response, our secular culture rebels against any kind of submission, of either gender, and tells us to prefer ourselves, to protect against abuse or manipulation. But we cannot risk the cost of rejecting the biblical design simply because some people do not follow it. When we look at the pure representation of this leadership, in the person and sacrifice of Jesus, we see anything but abuse; He poured out everything for His bride, embodying a clear call to lay down His life for her. This is our model for marriage—to surrender and yield to love, leaving the risk in God's hands.

A man is responsible to the Lord for how he loves his wife, and a woman answers to the Lord for how she honors her husband. When both husband and wife follow the call of God, their union causes both to flourish. In a healthy marriage, there is a great amount of influence flowing in both directions. One spouse does not control the other, but both can influence each other because of the desire to be connected. The design of marriage is a beautiful ebb and flow toward unity. Two people give themselves fully, but neither one disappears. Rather, a new thing, a new entity is created with a life of its own: the marriage. Together the marriage of a man and woman is more than the sum total of the two individuals. In the same way that a child is created from both a man and a woman without removing life from either, the marriage can be seen as having a separate life of its own, without depleting either individual. As the marriage is nurtured and tended, it grows. As it is neglected or wounded, it diminishes.

The fact that God chooses the marriage relationship to illustrate His connection to us, His Church, elevates the marriage relationship even further. This is not a man-made idea, with flaws or core deficiencies. It cannot be improved upon. This is a divine, holy union. Paul calls it a great mystery. In the final book of the Bible, Revelation, the Scriptures describe the marriage supper between Christ and the Church as the pinnacle of heaven and earth touching:

> *Then I heard again what sounded like the shout of a vast crowd or the roar of mighty ocean waves or the crash of loud thunder: 'Praise the Lord! For the Lord our God, the Almighty, reigns. Let us be glad and rejoice, and let us give honor to him. For the time has come for the wedding feast of the Lamb, and his bride has prepared herself. She has been given the finest of pure white linen to wear.'*
>
> *Revelation 19:6-8*

As we look at this overarching narrative of Scripture, from beginning to end, it is clear that marriage is something God created, celebrates, empowers, and protects. Because God values relationships so highly, He established boundaries for them, called covenants. These boundaries for marriage are essential and clear, laid out in Scripture from the beginning of time.

COVENANTS

One of the most important concepts in the Bible is that of covenants. Many people are familiar with the "New Covenant," but we see throughout Scripture that God initiates many covenants with His people. A covenant is an agreement or a contract between people, or between God and humans. These promises tie together the story of God with His people, Israel, and eventually reach out to the whole world through Jesus. Out of the nine covenants God makes with humans, only two are entirely irrevocable (to Abraham and Noah), meaning that God will fulfill His promise, whether or not humans meet the conditions of it. The other seven are considered *revocable* and God is only obligated to fulfill His obligations if mankind is obedient to the conditions attached to their agreement. If His people breach these conditions, God is not obligated to fulfill His part and the covenant no longer remains in effect. The fact that the covenants are revocable, or breakable, does not indicate that they are unimportant or invalid. God Himself initiated and entered into them, indicating their great importance and teaching us that an agreement can be revocable and still be holy and in God's will.

The marriage contract, made between a man and a woman before and with God, is modeled after these revocable covenants. It is sacred and binding and designed to last a lifetime, yet has requirements that, if not met, render it broken. This, of course, does not mean God takes these agreements lightly. It is precisely *because* He values them that He creates boundaries and clarity surrounding them.

In their book, "The Covenants", Kevin Conner and Ken Malmin write, "In order for a marriage covenant to be valid biblically, it must contain these three elements: calling, entering, and keeping."

Calling is the initiation, the choosing of the individuals, and the invitation into the covenant. In Scripture, God always takes the role of initiator. In a marriage, traditionally the man proposes to the woman, inviting her to join him in marriage. Their engagement is a mutual choosing of one another.

The *entering* is the response to the invitation. In Scripture, people must choose to enter into a covenant with God. This entering is marked by a further three elements: the words of the covenant, the blood of the covenant, and the seal of the covenant. Each covenant is unique and possesses its own symbolism. For instance, in the New Covenant, initiated by Jesus, the words of the covenant include the terms of repentance, faith, and obedience. The blood is the sacrifice of the body and blood of Jesus, and the seal, the Holy Spirit Himself.

In a wedding ceremony, both husband and wife are freely choosing to enter into the covenant of marriage, and we see these essential components symbolized in Christian weddings through the vows they take (the words), the rings they exchange (the seal), and their sexual union afterwards (the blood). These represent a holy, binding agreement that both people make to one another before God.

The *keeping* of the covenant is the final element of all revocable covenants. Once there has been a calling and an entering, both parties must keep the commitment they have made to one another by fulfilling the obligations they agreed to through the words of the covenant. God, of course, always keeps His word. That is never in question. However, we see that humans continually fail to, resulting in broken covenants throughout Scripture. In marriage, the keeping of the covenant is also required for the marriage to continue. When both husband and wife uphold their vows, the covenant is protected and preserved; when it is broken by one party, it is broken for both.

KEEPING OR BREAKING

Now, of course no husband or wife is perfect at upholding all the promises they made on their wedding day at all times. There are moments where we all fail to love or cherish each other. Does this mean the marriage covenant is broken from any and every shortcoming and sin? Not exactly. Our modern vows must be interpreted through a historical biblical lens for us to understand what God considers a breech in the contract.

During the time of the writing of Exodus, the marriage vows of the people of Israel included three things; food, clothing, and conjugal love (Exodus 21:10-11). These may seem odd to us as modern readers, but they represent principles that still hold fast today and are reflected in our common English vows, "to love, hold, and cherish." Withholding food or clothing would be a form of neglect, abandonment, and abuse, and perpetually withholding conjugal love, or giving it to someone else, is sexual unfaithfulness. Through the teachings of Moses, Jesus, and Paul, it is clear the marriage covenant *can* be broken by abuse and unfaithfulness, and that God allows for divorce in those instances as a mercy to the victim and a punishment to the perpetrator. When covenant is broken, it is the right of the victim to decide whether to divorce or not.

There are some in the church today who argue that marriage is permanent, no matter what, and divorce is not allowed, ever. I would encourage you to read "Divorce and Remarriage in the Church" by David Instone-Brewer, to get a deep understanding of the history of that assumption. The best biblical scholarship supports the view that the marriage covenant is revocable, and that divorce is both a God-given protection for the victim and a punishment for sin. This in no way devalues marriage. Rather, it protects it in the same way a business contract protects business. When I hire a professional and sign a contract, if they do not do the work by the deadline, the contract is broken and I am not obligated to pay. I, of course, have the choice to trust and give them a second chance if I want to, but once the contract is null and void, I am free to walk away. These contracts honor and value both parties and give protection in order for everyone to flourish.

It is important to note that the prophets viewed God's relationship with Israel as a marriage contract with stipulations, promises and penalties. If the stipulations were kept, they would enjoy the promise of a happy life together; if they were broken, the penalty was divorce. Of course, when we enter into a covenant—whether it's a marriage or a business contract—we do not desire the penalty. But the purpose of having a covenant agreement in the first place is protection; God values marriage so much that He safeguards it with a severe punishment if the relationship is not honored.

The moment your covenant was made, God championed your marriage. The vows made to you and to God by your husband on your wedding day were holy and binding, just as the vows you made were. God's desire was that your husband would serve you, care for you, lay down his life for you, and love you faithfully for the rest of your lives. Anything that deviates from that is outside of the will of God and is met with a fierce response from your protective Father.

PRAYER

God, thank You for creating and valuing marriage. Even though it hurts so deeply to think about all the ways my marriage fell short of Your design, I choose to trust that what You say about marriage is true. Help me to not lower my standards of marriage as I try to make sense of my life. Give me eyes to see the real thing, and to not settle for anything less. Thank You for valuing me so much that You require my husband to be faithful and loving. Help me now to value myself, and to follow You as You guide me.

APPLICATION

1. What does it mean to you that God uses marriage imagery to describe His relationship with His people?

2. How does understanding biblical covenants confirm or challenge your understanding of marriage?

3. Is there anything about God's original design and intentions for marriage that you hadn't previously understood? What does this new knowledge change for you?

Etched in stone
Scars
No going back to the
Smooth
    Clear
        Innocence

A Warrior
Nursing a babe
A fighter,
Wiping tears from the
Blue
    Eyed
        Collateral

Stepping over
Dead bodies of
Vows
    Memory
        Love

All is tinted and tainted
Shadow and filth
Lies
    Lies
        Lies

Limping
She trudges on
Sword of truth, shield of faith
Bleeding
    Moving
        Weeping

The Traitor
Cut through fair skin
Found the deepest place
The tender parts
Beautiful
    Naked
        Trust

Set it on fire
Walked away
Complaining of
Smoke
    Burning
        His eyes

This valley
Stretches endless
Reeks of
Death
    Waste
        Betrayal

She casts off
Clothes he gave
Cheap
To cover her
Truth
    Strength
        Power

Laid bare,
She is brilliant
Her scarred heart
Breaks open, spilling
Light
    Freedom
        Mercy

Justice rains down
Washing ash
And blood
Disintegrating
Lies
    Lies
        Lies

2

ADULTERY

GOD'S PERSPECTIVE

When I uncovered my husband's adultery, my world stood still. As the pieces of the previous months all clicked together in one illuminating, horrifying moment, I remember feeling and acting like a wild, wounded animal. I felt out of control, and yet the most awake I had been in a long time. A rage and indignation filled my bones, while my heart and hope were crushed into dust and lost in the wind; I had never been so angry.

I used to be alarmed when I read some of God's expressions of anger and judgment in the Old Testament, but then I found myself on a cool night, standing in a stranger's yard, screaming at a man I thought I knew, writhing in the deepest pain I could imagine, and in that moment, I understood God in a new and fresh way. *Of course* He was angry at His people, His bride! He loved her, and they had made covenant promises together. He had been deeply betrayed, as you and I have, and His response was as powerful as His love.

You might be surprised just how much God has to say about adultery throughout the Bible. Not only does He reference it often, but He condemns such betrayal with strong, visceral, and fierce language. God is the author of faithfulness and He abhors the perversion and destructiveness of unfaithfulness. He has endured it first-hand and seen the pain it inflicts upon His beloved people.

He has also seen *your* pain. You have not been hidden from Him, and He knows that as you embark on this journey toward healing, looking straight into your wound can be overwhelming and painful. While it is important to uncover the truth, my prayer is that you are surrounded by the comfort and love of God as you face this dark reality with Him. Take a moment to pause and ask Him to protect you as you read on. He understands how you feel.

ADULTERY CONDEMNED

To understand God's perspective on adultery, a read through the book of Proverbs, one of the wisdom books of Scripture, is a good place to start. It is frontloaded with numerous warnings against the danger and foolishness of infidelity. Rehearsing the themes from Genesis, Proverbs 5 begins with an overview of God's intended design for marriage: blessing, rejoicing, delight. This is what God created marriage to be—wonderful! Then the Scripture turns, warning against the trap of infidelity:

> *Let your fountain be blessed, and rejoice in the wife of your youth, a lovely deer, a graceful doe. Let her breasts fill you at all times with delight; be intoxicated always in her love. Why should you be intoxicated, my son, with a forbidden woman and embrace the bosom of an adulteress? For a man's ways are before the eyes of the Lord, and he ponders all his paths. The iniquities of the wicked ensnare him, and he is held fast in the cords of his sin. He dies for lack of discipline, and because of his great folly he is led astray.*
>
> Proverbs 5:18-23 (ESV)

This passage establishes several truths for us about what is going on in adultery, and why God hates it so much.

Adultery Involves Intoxication

Marriage itself is designed to be intoxicating—in a good way. As we see in the first half of the proverb, God designed for you to be the delight and source of intoxication for your husband and *he* is given the instruction to keep it that way. You are everything he needed. You are a gift and a blessing worth rejoicing over! This marital intoxication is beautiful and holy. Falling in love is a rush, and it is meant to be followed by standing in love and cultivating love for a lifetime.

God gave us wisdom in His Word before we had science to explain the power of falling in love, and now brain research supports what this proverb says. There are several biological responses in our bodies when we create romantic connections. When infatuation is pursued, norepinephrine signals excitement, dopamine sends a feel-good response, and serotonin levels drop, causing a visceral sense of longing. When sexual intimacy occurs, oxytocin floods the brain, causing deep emotional bonding. These biological responses were designed to bond two people together inside the safety of marriage. When you fell in love with your spouse, you were given the gift of this powerful concoction—you probably remember it well.

In adultery, however, these chemicals are twisted into a trap, perverting what was designed to ignite a life-long connection within a marriage into an unhealthy drug. It's the kind of intoxication that brings destruction. Just like any other drug or alcohol, adultery alters the cognitive capacity of the person engaging in it. The cocktail of chemicals in the brain of an adulterer are surprisingly powerful and addictive—as much as cocaine and amphetamines— and are increased by the element of secrecy.[1] It is important to understand just how powerful the intoxication is that your husband is under. The impact on him is like it is for anyone who is under the influence of drugs or alcohol, however, your adulterous husband is still completely responsible for his actions and their consequences. His 'substance abuse' is forbidden and has no excuse.

---

1. https://aboutaffairs.com/2016/03/what-happens-to-the-brain-during-an-affair/

Adultery is Forbidden by God

Proverbs 5 makes it clear that adultery is an iniquity, a sin. Another woman is forbidden and the man engaging in this sin is called "wicked" (v.22). There is no excuse for this sin, or any other. No matter what your adulterous husband says or feels, the Bible continually paints a picture of how much God values marriage, and detests unfaithfulness. In all of Scripture, *there is never a valid excuse for adultery.* Rather, there is a stark warning that God abhors this sexual sin and views it as an affront to His design.

Remember, the Bible uses marital language to describe Jesus' relationship with the Church which shows us how strongly God treasures marriage. In contrast to this biblical value of fidelity and covenant commitment, the ethos of our culture is sexual fluidity, boundary-less pleasure seeking, and freedom from restraints. *Do what feels good. Live out your truth. The heart wants what the heart wants,* are the sentiments we are told to live by. These cultural values place an individual at the center of their own reality and morality, allowing them to define life based on their own desires without restraints. God rejects this dangerous mindset that deceives so many and leads to sin like adultery. His high value for marriage is exactly *why* He has an equally passionate revulsion to the perversion of infidelity.

The biblical worldview offers us freedom *inside* of the restraints of covenant that protect and clarify relationships. Every command given in Scripture is given for our benefit. Any time God forbids something, He does so out of His love and wisdom. This means He forbids this sin because He loves both you and your husband and does not want you or him to be destroyed by wickedness. God honors the marriage covenant, not the desires of the flesh, and therefore, He will not accept or consider any excuse your husband may make for his actions. Under no circumstances will God bless an affair. God's love says "no" to this choice.

Adultery Will be Exposed

One of the initial stings of finding out about an affair is the knowledge that you've been in the dark; the shame and confusion is overwhelming. There is so much that you don't know, that you've been lied to about, and you cannot know with certainty what really happened, or when. Be assured that God knows. Nothing is hidden from the Lord's sight, and He sees every step that has led to this place of sin.

Not only does He know every detail, but He is also a just and righteous judge. What you are walking through is *not fair*. Your husband may not be taking responsibility, people may not believe you, and you may be faced with all sorts of other injustices. Take heart, sister. God sees it all. When it comes to ultimate justice, your husband will not be getting away with anything. We are all accountable for our actions, and God will bring to light every sin that your husband has committed against you. In the Gospel of Luke, Jesus tells His followers, "For all that is secret will eventually be brought into the open, and everything that is concealed will be brought to light and made known to all" (Luke 8:17).

The 'eventually' can be difficult for us to accept. I know the desperate desire to learn the truth, with all the necessary details, *now*. I, too, had to learn to trust God's timing. It was only as I witnessed how He orchestrated all the events in order for me to uncover my husband's affair that I began to understand and was able to trust that He would continue to shine light on the things I needed to know in due time. Likewise, God is advocating and orchestrating justice for you. You can trust His timing and know that His anger burns against the wrongs committed against you.

Adultery Ends in Bondage

The path to adultery is a choice made willingly, but once someone makes the choice to travel down that path, there is a spiritual stronghold created by this sin. It is a trap and a snare, and the adulterer becomes a slave. It is important to recognize that your husband walked into this sin knowingly. While he opened a door to a strong evil that will not be easy for him to escape, that is not an excuse for his initial decision. He *sold himself* into slavery.

This might seem like a harsh statement, but Scripture is clear that while temptation may be strong, it can be withstood. Paul tells us, "No temptation has overtaken you that is not common to man. God is faithful, and he will not let you be tempted beyond your ability, but with the temptation he will also provide the way of escape, that you may be able to endure it" (1 Corinthians 10:13, ESV). Your husband rejected the way of escape and walked straight into captivity.

While it is imperative to know that your husband alone is responsible for his choices, it is also vital to understand there is an enemy at work here who is not your husband. This enemy has been empowered by your husband's choices. From the outset of the book of Genesis, we see a demonic agenda to tempt humans to follow Satan and become his slaves. When people choose sin rather than obedience to God, the evil one grows in power. That power is now working against your husband, and it will be much more difficult for him to walk out of bondage than it was for him to walk into it. He may not even realize or acknowledge that he is bound, but God's Word does not lie. Infidelity is a prison that your husband has locked himself into, and he no longer has the key. He will need God's Spirit to release him. You did not lead him into bondage, you did not lock him up, and you cannot get him out. That is out of your hands.

Adultery Leads to Death

Adultery murders a marriage. The consequence is real. It breaks the covenant. It is not merely damaged, or strained—it is broken. This is why there is such devastation and trauma for you. There is more than just a relational challenge to overcome; there has been a death that must be processed and grieved. I am not saying there is no hope. With God, a miracle can take place. Perhaps a resurrection can occur, or a new marriage begin. I have seen it happen. Yet even when a marital resurrection has taken place, it is important to still acknowledge that what was *dead* is now alive. That is what makes it a miracle. But whether there is repentance and restoration or not, it helps no one to avoid the hard truth: Infidelity kills a marriage.

The cause of death is the lack of discipline of the adulterer. It is very likely your husband will try to blame you or ask you to share the burden of responsibility for this death, but Scripture tells us that the path *he chose* is what leads to death. In another proverb warning against adultery, the writer implores his sons to stay away from an adulterous woman:

> *Let not your heart turn aside to her ways, do not stray into her paths, for many a victim has she laid low, and all her slain are a mighty throng. Her house is the way to Sheol, going down to the chambers of death.*
>
> *Proverbs 7:25-27 (ESV)*

The warning could not be clearer: this road leads to death. Words like *Sheol*, 'the place of the dead', and 'slain' imply the right kind of heaviness and severity that is a consequence of infidelity. The Bible firmly teaches that sexual sin leads to an individual's death and prevents people from entering into the Kingdom of God (1 Corinthians 6:9-11, Galatians 5:19-20). Of course, if someone repents and is washed, justified, and sanctified by Jesus, they will be saved. But the risk to someone's soul is very great when they engage in adultery.

These strong warnings in Scripture validate why adultery hurts so deeply and remind us once again that God takes faithfulness very seriously. Your marriage was valuable and meaningful and cherished by God. He is the One who created and initiated covenant, and He defends it fiercely. Your marriage was designed to bless you, and God is protective not only of it, but also of you. He gave unequivocal instructions to your husband, and your husband disobeyed the Lord. While you are suffering because of his choices, please know that God does not hold you responsible for his infidelity. You can remain under God's covering, regardless of your husband's choices. God knows what it is to be faithful in the face of great unfaithfulness.

GOD'S MARRIAGE AND DIVORCE

I read my Bible with fresh eyes after experiencing infidelity. The way God used marital language to help us understand His desire for His people stood out to me in a way it hadn't previously—as did His emotions when they were unfaithful. This wasn't just something God warned us against as humans. He experienced it too. He knows our pain.

Human marriage can never fully illustrate the connection between God and His people. After all, God is divine and perfect, whereas in a human marriage, both individuals are mortal and imperfect. However, it is no mistake that God chose this kind of language to help us understand the importance of faithfulness to Him. God chose marriage to communicate the depth of His commitment and, likewise, the depth of His emotions when He is betrayed.

The most prominent sin that God warns against and hates is idolatry. In His Ten Commandments to the people of Israel, idolatry was dealt with first. When God's people pursued other gods and worshipped idols, the language of infidelity was used to describe their sin. God's response to their unfaithfulness was that of an angry, wounded, and wronged spouse as we see when God reveals His heart to the prophet Jeremiah:

> *Have you seen what faithless Israel has done? She has gone up on every high hill and under every spreading tree and has committed adultery there. I thought that after she had done all this she would return to me but she did not, and her unfaithful sister Judah saw it. I gave faithless Israel her certificate of divorce and sent her away because of all her adulteries.*
>
> *Jeremiah 3:6-8 (NIV)*

God deemed Israel's worship of other gods—at the altars in the high places—an act of adultery. God thought Israel would return, and indeed called her to. We see there a model for potential reconciliation, a miraculous relational resurrection. But we also see that when the requirements for reconciliation were not met, God gave Israel her certificate of divorce. Again, God takes this seriously. His act of divorcing Israel was a just and righteous response. Anyone who claims that a victim of infidelity who gets divorced is in sin, needs to read Jeremiah and make that same claim against a holy God. *Divorce is a response to sin, but is not necessarily a sin in and of itself.* To argue otherwise is to claim that God sinned against Israel, which is preposterous.

Israel's actions brought on a strong response from God—they also caused visceral feelings in Him. In Deuteronomy, Moses describes those feelings like this:

> *They **stirred up his jealousy** by worshiping foreign gods; they **provoked his fury** with detestable deeds.*
>
> *Deuteronomy 32:16 (emphasis mine)*

God was furious, enraged by their unfaithfulness. The kind of anger and jealousy you have felt, God understands. You do not have to be ashamed of those same emotions. They are appropriate; God has felt them too.

Also remember, your husband entered into a covenant with you *before God*. He has not only violated you, but he has also violated God. You are not alone in your jealousy and rage. God's righteous anger burns against what has been done to you and Him.

GROUNDS FOR DIVORCE, GRACE FOR RECONCILIATION

Anger is not an emotion that we are built to sustain, and we see that while God certainly gets angry, He does not remain so indefinitely. Like many who have been violated, there was a period of time where He considered restoration. In order for any restoration to be possible, however, He required true repentance. And so, He issued this invitation to Israel:

> *O Israel, my faithless people, come home to me again, for I am merciful. I will not be angry with you forever. Only acknowledge your guilt. Admit that you rebelled against the LORD your God and committed adultery against him by worshiping idols under every green tree. Confess that you refused to listen to my voice. I, the LORD, have spoken!*
>
> *Jeremiah 3:12-13*

God called Israel back to Himself. But first He required repentance, confession, and an acknowledgment of guilt from her. It was not a suggestion, it was essential. Reconciliation could not happen without a true turning back toward Him. God called Israel home, but she chose not to return.

It is worth pausing here to mention that my hope and prayer is that your husband *will* return, repent, confess, and acknowledge his grievous sin. If he were to do that, *and* you feel led to reconcile, I believe that God can help you heal together and create a new covenant to replace the one that has been destroyed. When someone returns to God, He is able to work miracles of restoration and reconciliation. If you have reconciled, or are on that journey, please know that I am cheering for you. This was my desire for my marriage, and I took steps to create a pathway home for my husband, but he chose not to walk down that road with me.

I share my experience with divorce as descriptive, not prescriptive. What God did in my life displays His glory, but it's never meant to be a 'should' for someone else's story. God will be glorified by your obedience to Him, whatever that looks like, and He will lead you each step as you follow, whether your husband is repentant or not. Unfortunately, my husband's repentance was not genuine, and sadly, this is the most common outcome when an affair has taken place. God speaks of insincere repentance in reference to Judah,

Israel's sister nation:

> *"And I saw that for all the adulteries of faithless Israel, I had sent her away and given her a certificate of divorce, yet her treacherous sister Judah did not fear; but she went and prostituted herself also. And because of the thoughtlessness of her prostitution, she defiled the land and committed adultery with stones and trees. Yet in spite of all this her treacherous sister **Judah did not return to Me with all her heart, but rather in deception,**" declares the Lord.*
>
> *Jeremiah 3:8-10 (NASB, emphasis mine)*

It is possible for an adulterer to appear to return and repent, but to do it in deception. This is not acceptable to the Lord and it should not be acceptable to you. If your husband is not truly repentant, do not allow him to return home to you. I know that it can be very difficult to discern if he's being genuine, and I pray that you are able to see and accept the truth, no matter what it is.

I do not know what the outcome of your marriage will be. All I can encourage you to do is to seek God and follow His leading. Know that if God calls you to remain, He will strengthen you, but also know that Scripture does not require you to endure this kind of violation. God allows for divorce only under extreme circumstances, and unfaithfulness is extreme; God takes it very seriously. Jesus says twice in the book of Matthew that adultery is grounds for divorce (Matthew 5:32, 19:9). Of course, His desire and instruction were that marriage should be held in the highest honor so that no one would experience infidelity, or divorce as its consequence—He commanded men to keep their eyes and their thoughts pure, and to turn their affections to their wives only. Jesus was certainly pro-marriage, and as a divorced woman, so am I. But Jesus also recognized that adultery breaks the covenant, rendering the marriage destroyed. It was never God's intention for marriage to be defiled like this, but in His mercy, He has made a way out for those who need it. My heart, and I believe God's heart, is to see you heal, whether you are with your husband or not.

As I have said before, there is no one-size-fits all formula for what a marriage looks like after infidelity. As we saw in Scripture, God divorced His people for their covenant-breaking infidelity, and Jesus' teaching confirmed that such a response is acceptable (Matthew 5:31-32). Yet the book of Hosea reveals that there are times when God calls for a long-suffering waiting and redemption that goes beyond common sense or natural abilities. Hosea's commitment to his unfaithful, prostituting wife was a powerful prophetic picture that God was going to redeem a remnant of Israel and fulfill His *irrevocable covenant* with Abraham. God promised there would be a day beyond His divorce of Israel when He would make a New Covenant with His unfaithful people through Jesus, who is faithful on our behalf. Of course, even under the New Covenant, the people of Israel had a choice to accept Jesus as Messiah or not, and many chose to be cut off. Just as He has done from the very beginning, God continues to allow us to choose union with Him or not.

There is a mystery here, and only God Himself can reveal His heart for your story. And while the example of Hosea is not a binding command for everyone to remain with an unfaithful spouse, we should all have the humility to acknowledge that God alone has the right to tell a victim to stay or go. God often told His prophets to do extreme, out-of-the-ordinary things, like telling Ezekiel to eat food cooked over dung (Ezekiel 4:12). These were real instructions to real people, but they were obviously not general commands for all God's people, for all time. There are actually no commands to divorce in Scripture, and no commands to remain married after infidelity. What we *are* commanded to do is to submit our lives unto the Lord and follow the leading of His Spirit, in accordance with His Word.

After my husband's affair came to light, I sensed God was asking me to wait for a specific period of time—ninety days—before making any decisions, and I obeyed. I was determined to heal, and if there was a chance I could *heal with him*, then I wanted to be able to know in my heart and tell my children that I had allowed space for that and given it my very best. I wanted to give my husband the opportunity to wake up and turn. Once that time was up, however, and my husband continued to lie, blame, and cheat, I felt fully released to heal without him. I am so grateful that I listened to God's leading to wait, *and* His leading to go. His timing is perfect.

I know godly women who have waited years by the call of the Lord, and women who did not wait at all. I believe these women followed the specific call of God on their lives, and trust that God will also speak to you. If you are unsure of what He is saying yet, I urge you to wait until you hear clearly before making any big decisions. His protective Father heart wants to guard you from further damage and lead you into healing and restoration as His precious daughter.

PRAYER

God, thank You for showing me how You feel about adultery. Israel's unfaithfulness was not Your fault, and my husband's unfaithfulness is not my fault. Help me to believe it. Give me discernment to see true repentance from false repentance and give me patience and wisdom as I wait on You. Thank You that You understand my anger, my jealousy, and my pain. Keep me from sin as I process these emotions and help me to clearly hear Your instructions. I trust in Your timing and Your heart for me.

APPLICATION

1. What feelings rise up in you as you read Proverbs 5?

2. How does thinking of God's marriage and divorce in the Old Testament shape your perspective on your own situation?

3. What actions, if any, by your husband might indicate repentance? What actions might indicate false repentance?

The mountain
Every morning, the mountain

Some days I get to the top
Early, easily
Enjoying the view
Legs strong
Lungs full

Adorned with jewelry
Forged from the silver lining,
I conquer the hell
Out of this hill

Not today

The clouds are not silver-lined
They are B<small>LACK</small>
The mud is slick
My feet slip and sink

The icy rain
Mixes with the ghost of my tears
I can't even cry anymore

No one can lift me
It is my mountain alone

So
Alone

If my anger could fuel my drive
I would stand and try again
But it brought despair along

What is THE POINT?

I am sick of this
The survival is getting old
Grief is too long, too deep

People treat me like
Some sort of hero
And maybe I am

But today?
I don't want to be inspiring
I want to be LOVED

Fought for
Adored
Celebrated
Touched
Seen

The rain pounds
There is no one here
Love is not my story

Muddy fingers clutch for a hold
Eyes look up to dark, spewing heavens
"Help me!"

Not a sweet request
Not a trusting expectation
This is a demand
I am Jacob, and we wrestle,
You and I

BLESS ME
Do it now
I am desperate and unafraid
Meet me, fight me, wreck me

I'll take the limp

3

SUFFERING

NEARNESS TO GOD

Experiencing the devastation of an affair causes an unspeakably deep suffering. In the weeks and months after my husband's infidelity was exposed, my body and brain were wracked with pain. I had never experienced anguish and torment like that, and it was disorienting. Yet life kept coming at me. It seemed cruel to have to continue to do normal things—to still have to eat, pay bills, bathe my kids, wash the dishes, parent. Most of those early days felt impossible; the pain was all-consuming.

In the West, we tend to have a very stunted understanding of suffering. Modern advancements and the relative affluence of our culture have eliminated enough pain that we often do not know how to properly process it when it comes. Now, I'm not suggesting that easing discomfort is a bad thing. I believe God is pleased when we make choices that bring wholeness rather than perpetuating brokenness. However, I think that as Christians, we are at risk of missing a key component of the Gospel if we expect a victory-only, pain-free version of life as we follow God. We need a theology of suffering—one that allows us to face our pain and gives us permission to ask our questions.

This was my journey. I certainly was not living a pain-free life, and I had to wrestle with why.

WHY IS THIS HAPPENING?

Some people feel that their marriage was a mistake from the beginning. Perhaps you entered into the marriage out of rebellion, foolishness, or disobedience to the Lord. Only you can really know where your heart was when you made that commitment. Regardless of the state of your heart on your wedding day, the vows that were made were holy and binding. To say the whole marriage was a mistake would be to partner with the lie that your husband was justified in violating it. After all, if the marriage was worthless and doomed to fail, it lessens the crime of ending it, right? The truth is, your marriage was valuable and had everything needed to succeed; it was alive, and to kill it was a crime. I believe this is true of every marriage. Even if it started out of sin, God's grace makes space for every marriage to be whole and holy if both people choose that.

But that's the key: *We get to choose.*

I know that I was obedient to the Lord and submitted to His Spirit when I chose to commit myself to my husband in marriage. From that day forward, I chose life for us. My husband had that same power, but he chose death. And when he did, the suffering that followed for me was the consequence of his choices. It was not the result of my own sin, nor was it sent from God; it was the fruit of how my husband chose to use his free will to pursue sin. I do not believe he was destined to choose this path, but he certainly was allowed to.

I had to wrestle with that. I knew God didn't *make* him do it, but He *let* him. How was I supposed to feel about that? I wish I could say God gave me a clear-cut answer that I could now pass on to you, but the truth is that when we come to God with our questions, what heals us most is not an answer, but being *with* Him.

It is okay to grapple with the question of "Why?" *Why me? Why now? Why this?* All throughout Scripture we hear God's people crying out, looking for answers to the deep questions of suffering and injustice.

In fact, not only does God allow us to wrestle and lament, He wrote it into His Word, making it a holy act of engaging with Him. As we see in the book of Job, wrestling can lead us into an encounter with God. Just as with Job, God may not give us a clear answer, but His presence will change us and teach us how to steward the painful gift of grief, bringing meaning into our suffering.

Along with the book of Proverbs, Job and Ecclesiastes are also classified as wisdom literature in Scripture. Proverbs is easily recognizable as such, giving us solid 'how-to's' to improve our chance of a whole life. But anyone who has lived long understands that while that wisdom is a true and sure guide, it does not and cannot prevent all pain and hardship from entering our lives. Ecclesiastes and Job are our guides into wrestling with that reality. If Proverbs is a 'how-to', then Ecclesiastes is a 'how-come', and Job a 'what-now'. It is significant that two thirds of wisdom literature does not give us answers, but rather permission to wrestle with our questions, and ultimately invites us to surrender to mystery and trust. These books offer us hope that while God's wisdom may not always prevent suffering or answer the question "Why?" in human terms, it is applicable in every circumstance and will shape us for the better if we will trust in the Lord and in His ways.

I do not have a simple or clear explanation of why this has happened to you. I believe that in this lifetime, there are mysteries too hidden for us to fully comprehend until we are made whole with resurrection life. But I do know that, in this season of your life, how you engage with your suffering will determine your healing on this dark road.

Scripture gives us instructions on what to do *when* we suffer. This means that it cannot be avoided. You did not do something wrong to make this happen, nor is there any way to avoid all pain in life. The fact that some measure of hardship is expected for us also means that God is not defeated when we encounter it on this earth. In fact, it is through adversity that God often turns what the enemy meant for evil into something truly good. God Himself suffered, and through His suffering He not only identifies with our pain, but conquers it. The cross is our proof of this. What looks like bad news is what we call the Good News. The climax of the Gospel is a death.

THE CROSS

Sometimes we look at the cross and mistakenly think that Jesus was just murdered; that the cross was simply a misfortune on the way to resurrection—the enemy won for a moment, and then God quickly made a 'Plan B', snatching up the victory in the last minute. But the truth is, from the beginning of time, God ordained salvation, healing, restoration, and an eternal covenant to be birthed *through suffering* (Acts 2:23). His own suffering. The cross was not a pit stop on the way to victory. *The cross was the victory.* The resurrection was the sign and testimony that Jesus had triumphed over sin and death, but the war itself was won on the cross.

Jesus led the way to victory through suffering. His choice to surrender His life and die in our place means that God's presence was brought into the process of suffering and dying. He claimed the rights over that territory. No longer is suffering only a weapon of the enemy against the people of God. In Christ, sorrow is now turned around into a weapon against darkness; the cross is the ultimate display of this.

In Colossians 2 we read, "And having disarmed the powers and authorities, he made a public spectacle of them, triumphing over them by the cross" (v.15, NIV). The cross was not the defeat of Yahweh, it was His victory. The cross was not a failure of God's goodness and faithfulness, it was the perfect picture of it. The cross was not a waste, it was the purpose of Christ from before time began.

When we have a right view of the cross and the agony of Christ, we have the chance to see how God wants to infuse our own afflictions with purpose. When our pain is wrapped up in the presence of

God, it becomes priceless. You know how much this season is costing you—I assure you, the price you are paying does not need to be in vain.

Of course, just as with all of our lives, we have the freedom to choose. Our suffering can either be surrendered to God or not. We can hold onto our hurt and exclude God from the process, but if we do, it will lead to more anguish—perhaps even permanent damage. We see this throughout our world: People get hurt, and they hurt others, and the cycle of sin and abuse continues. However, when we choose to invite God into our struggle and surrender it into His hands, He transforms us, bringing more wholeness and life than there was before. On the cross, Jesus purchased purpose for our pain. This is the work of our God, ushering in new creation, even now, even in this darkness.

PURPOSE IN SUFFERING

Of course, one might ask, "Doesn't the Bible say there will be no pain or tears in the new heaven and the new earth?" Yes—it does! In the closing chapters of Revelation, we read:

> *He will wipe away every tear from their eyes, and death shall be no more, neither shall there be mourning, nor crying, nor pain anymore, for the former things have passed away.*
>
> *Revelation 21:4 (ESV)*

We all long for this day. There is so much comfort in knowing that our suffering will end; that there will come a time when our hearts will no longer ache.

However, just because pain and tears will not come with us into the fully established Kingdom of God does not mean that they are inherently evil and have no place in His Kingdom now. Just as in the new heaven and earth there will no longer be pain or tears, there will also be no more prophecy or hope. This is not because prophecy and hope are bad—they are wonderful! We just will not need those things in the new creation, because we will live in perfect union with God and all He has promised to us will be fully realized. Certainly, prophecy and hope are gifts to us now. Mysteriously, pain and tears are gifts to us now as well. They will not be required once we have our resurrected bodies, and I know none of us will miss them, but they are needed on this earth. They have a place and a purpose.

To be fair, I do not know anyone who enjoys hurting or crying. However, we have all likely had an experience where the tears welled up in our eyes, and someone said, "Stop crying!" In that moment, something inside caves in, with instant shame and deepened hurt. This kind of dismissive response to pain can be more damaging than the pain itself, and we know instinctively that it isn't quite right. Putting on a happy face when our heart is broken makes us weary and disconnected. There is a cruelty in fake joy that is not found in honest hurt. We were meant to live in the truth. We were built for it. So, when something false is laid on us, it just doesn't fit right. The truth is that the world we live in has brokenness that deserves pain and tears, and sometimes, sorrow is the most honoring and honest response we can give.

We often read of lepers in the Bible, but many of us may not have a context of what that awful disease does. Thankfully, today it is fairly rare and more easily treated than previously, but one read through the New Testament and you can see how devastating it was back then and how much fear there was surrounding it. Leprosy is a long-term infection that damages the nerves, among other areas of the body. This nerve damage causes a person to not be able to feel pain. You may think that sounds amazing right about now, and I get it! Pain feels wrong. But in reality, pain is not wrong itself, it is simply *a signal of what is wrong*. Without this signal, people with leprosy cannot feel when they get wounded, and as a result, they often lose body parts because their injuries and infections go undetected. Without pain, they cannot feel when they are experiencing damage. In the same way, when we feel emotional pain, it is a warning to us that something else is very, very wrong.

It is important to mention here that while pain does have a purpose, this does not mean that you are called to endure continued abuse or sin from another person, unless it is for the sake of the gospel. Suffering has been over-spiritualized by some, and its value should not be used as a manipulative tool to keep people trapped in sinful, hurtful situations. Yes, God allowed your husband to choose, and his detestable choice hurt you. But God also allows *you* to choose. While you cannot escape all the pain caused from the affair, you have the choice to protect yourself as much as you can from further violation. It is okay to move away from the fire. Scripture supports boundaries. We are told to not even associate with certain types of unrepentant people, and to not waste our value and virtue (1 Corinthians 5:11, Matthew 7:6).

The root of all that is wrong in the world is sin. This sounds elementary, but it reveals that suffering itself is not what needs to be dealt with. Pain is not wrong, sin is. So often, the world wants to eliminate what hurts without recognizing that we must deal with the fire before we can prevent the burn. The pain is a signal, the suffering is a signal, and until sin is completely gone, and the full reign of Christ is established on the earth, we need these things to be our nerve endings, guiding us away from the flames.

Not only does pain communicate something to us, but it also produces something in us. Paul reminds the hurting church in Rome, "Suffering produces endurance, and endurance produces character, and character produces hope, and hope does not put us to shame, because God's love has been poured into our hearts through the Holy Spirit who has been given to us" (Romans 5:3-5, ESV).

If you are anything like me, I have often read that and thought, *No, thanks. I don't think I want any more endurance or character, thank you very much.* But as Christ followers, we are not only being rescued from sin and death, we are also being formed into the very nature of Christ. *This is the whole purpose of the Christian life,* to become like Him who has saved us. We are called to nothing less than the agony of a crucified life, and nothing less than the glory of the resurrection. This does not mean that the cause of our suffering is anything that God condones, but He is certain to use it to shape us into Jesus' image, and to turn it into a weapon against darkness.

God not only promises to comfort and deliver you, but He intends to equip you to comfort others. Paul, after enduring many beatings and imprisonments, sends this encouragement to the church in Corinth:

> *Praise be to the God and Father of our Lord Jesus Christ, the Father of compassion and the God of all comfort, who comforts us in all our troubles, so that we can comfort those in any trouble with the comfort we ourselves receive from God. For just as we share abundantly in the sufferings of Christ, so also our comfort abounds through Christ.*
>
> 2 Corinthians 1:3-5 (NIV)

I cannot express how grateful I am to know that God has not allowed the agony from my husband's affair to go to waste but has equipped me to comfort many women in a way most others cannot. There will be a day when the pain you are walking through becomes hope and comfort for another. You may not be there yet, but I promise that it is coming.

Be assured that this is not some cold math equation where "you plus suffering equals a better you." No, it is deeper and more mysterious than that. God is not just trying to teach you an important lesson, like some stony, aloof teacher. He has *entered in with you*. Just as He took your sin on the cross, Jesus also bore your grief (Isaiah 53:4). He has carried, and is currently carrying, your pain from the affair with you. He not only catches your tears; they mix with His own.

SUFFERING WITH GOD

How beautiful that God does not abandon us to experience our suffering and weakness alone, but rather comes alongside us in it. The incarnation, Jesus becoming embodied in the flesh, and entering into our frailty and vulnerability, is almost unthinkably wonderful. He did not have to do it; He chose to come hurt with us. When you are in pain, He sympathizes with you. Jesus is the One who wept.

I often marvel at the account of Jesus mourning at the tomb of Lazarus (John 11:35). His dear friend had died, and Jesus knew that He was moments from resurrecting him. However, He did not instruct Lazarus' friends and family to stop their grieving. Rather, He ached and cried with them. Certainly, if grief could be, or should be avoided, Jesus would have said so then. Heaven was about to break into earth, life was about to overcome death. And yet, Jesus wept. Honest and open suffering does not mean you lack faith, hope, or trust in the Lord. It just means it hurts. God knows, understands, and enters into that hurt with you.

This is not the only time in Scripture where we encounter Jesus as our weeping Savior. In Hebrews we read:

> *While Jesus was here on earth, he offered prayers and pleadings, with a loud cry and tears, to the one who could rescue him from death. And God heard his prayers because of his deep reverence for God. Even though Jesus was God's Son, he learned obedience from the things he suffered.*
>
> *Hebrews 5:7-8*

Jesus cried out, pleaded with God, weeping and calling out for rescue. Does that sound familiar? Yet notice the hope in His tears: God heard Him. And when you cry out, God hears you also.

Jesus suffered, and He not only endured it, but learned obedience through it. This word 'obedience' in Greek is *hupakoé*, meaning 'submission to what is heard'. In order to obey, Jesus had to posture Himself to hear. Suffering caused Jesus to be more in tune with the Father's voice. The Father responded to Jesus' cries, just as Jesus responded to God's words. This beautiful, yet painful, access to hearing and submitting is something that is available to us as well.

We have the opportunity to cry out, lean in, and hear God's response to us, and as we learn to obey His voice, we are transformed more and more into the likeness of Jesus.

But in this process of surrender, God does not expect you to enjoy suffering. Jesus endured emotional and physical pain before His betrayal, torture, and death. He knew it was coming and agonized over it. He sweat tears of blood in the garden of Gethsemane, asking God to remove the cup of suffering from Him. He cried out to our Father to spare Him, to make it go away (Luke 22:42). Ultimately, He trusted and surrendered, but be encouraged that even Jesus struggled with accepting the suffering before Him. The path before you is lined with hardship, no matter which way you turn. It is okay if you struggle to accept it, as Jesus did. His mercy, patience, and compassion are still surrounding you.

We often focus on the gift Jesus gave us in His willingness to suffer, die, and conquer on our behalf. That is worth our wonder and worship, forever. But what a gift Jesus also gave the Father in that moment, presenting Him with a profound trust in His goodness and promises in the midst of His suffering.

Since my best days still fall short of what He deserves, I have often wondered what I could possibly offer God. I will never forget the revelation that the greatest gift I can give Him is my loyalty, surrender, and trust during my darkest hour. We will share an eternity in everlasting light, where I will see plainly His glory, and experience fully His goodness. It is only now, in this mortal life, in this suffering life, that I am able to give Him the gift of trusting in the dark. It is not easy, and that is why it is such a potent offering.

You may cry, as Jesus did, "Father, why have you forsaken me?" (Matthew 27:46). But Jesus was quoting Psalm 22, and as is so common in the psalms, the cry of suffering and questioning is eventually followed with statements of faith and confidence in God's goodness. The end of Psalm 22 reveals a deep trust in God's nearness, and an honor for His goodness:

> *Praise the Lord, all you who fear him! Honor him, all you descendants of Jacob! Show him reverence, all you descendants of Israel! For he has not ignored or belittled the suffering of the needy. He has not turned his back on them, but has listened to their cries for help.*
>
> *Psalm 22:23-24*

God is not ignoring you—you have His attention. Nor is He belittling your suffering, He validates and acknowledges how much pain you are in. He will not turn His back on you; even now He is bending down, drawing near to you. God is listening to your cries for help, so keep calling out with the knowledge that just as His suffering and death were not final, your suffering is not final either. With God's covering, it will lead you into a new season of life and power that you could never have imagined possible.

SUFFERING WELL

We know that trials are inevitable, valuable even, and that God is with us, participating in our suffering. But what are we supposed to do with this pain? Is all suffering the same? Or is our posture, our response, important? Scripture shows us that God wants to work something beautiful in us *through* our suffering, and while He does the heavy lifting of accomplishing that work, our cooperation matters. The apostle Peter encourages us with these words:

> *Beloved, do not be surprised at the fiery ordeal among you, which comes upon you for your testing, as though something strange were happening to you; but* **to the degree that you share the sufferings of Christ, keep on rejoicing,** *so that at the revelation of His glory you may also rejoice and be overjoyed... Therefore, those also who suffer according to the will of God are to entrust their souls to a faithful Creator in doing what is right.*
>
> *1 Peter 4:12-13, 19 (NASB, emphasis mine)*

Rejoicing? Really? Is that even possible?

It is.

Rejoicing in suffering is an act and a proof of the grace of God. It defies all reason and is a powerful display of the Spirit of the Living God in the life of the believer. To say, "Even now, even here, I trust You," is the most powerful declaration of faith a follower of Christ can make. We are not rejoicing because we enjoy adversity itself, we are rejoicing that we get to touch Jesus, and His suffering. We get to understand the disappointment, the betrayal, the pain that our Savior endured for us, and to have the weighty privilege of bonding with Him in grief.

In verse 19, Peter tells the church that they "are to entrust their souls to a faithful Creator in doing what is right." This is how we entrust our souls, ourselves, to God in testing times: *By doing what is right.*

You mean God expects us to do the right thing, and obey Him, even though these other people are clearly in the wrong?

Yes, beloved. That is what God expects. Not because He wants to burden you, but because He longs to *protect* you. The safest place for you is in the middle of His way, on the path He sets out in His Word. He is faithful, and there will be a revelation of His glory that will cause you great joy and celebration. But you must stay close to Him to see it.

Not only do we get to connect with God in a profound way in the midst of pain, but there is a real fruit that is produced. There are real gifts and promises that come to us when we suffer well with Him. Further on in Peter's letter he tells us:

> And after you have suffered a little while, the God of all grace, who has called you to his eternal glory in Christ, **will himself restore, confirm, strengthen, and establish you.**
>
> *1 Peter 5:10 (ESV, emphasis mine)*

The aching heart of someone who is suffering longs for these things—restoration, confirmation, strength, being established, experiencing *life*. The Lord knows that this is what you need, sister, and this is the hope you are promised. It is not easy, it is not cheap, but it is yours. It belongs to you, as you suffer close to the heart of God. The victory and healing that your heart desires is on this very path that hurts so much. The pain is not the final destination. Because suffering costs so much, there will be a reward. As Paul reminds us, it will not be wasted:

> *We are afflicted in every way, but not crushed; perplexed, but not driven to despair; persecuted, but not forsaken; struck down, but not destroyed; always carrying in the body the death of Jesus,* **so that the life of Jesus may also be manifested in our bodies.**
>
> *2 Corinthians 4:8-10 (ESV, emphasis mine)*

There is a mystery in the connection between the death and life of Jesus that we carry with us. The "so that" means that His death was a necessary means to produce His life in us. There was purpose in His death, and though you may not see it, or even want it, there is purpose in your loss during this season. If you will allow God to touch your pain, He can use it to strengthen and establish you. In the midst of my deepest agony, I found a bedrock of determination; the enemy had done his worst, but I was still committed to Jesus, who was manifest in me. He restored me, and His life carried me through the death of my marriage.

It takes great faith to trust God in the middle of the storm. I know that you may not feel hope or strength or even God Himself; you may only feel death. But suffering well does not mean changing how you feel, it just means choosing to connect with God right where you are. He heals everything we let Him touch. Allow Jesus to touch even this and to bring it purpose.

PRAYER

God, I do not want this suffering. I do not understand it. But I know that You understand what it is to suffer, and I thank You for being with me in this. You did not ever have to suffer, but You chose to, for my sake. Help me to choose to invite You into my pain and not shut You out. It hurts so badly, and in the moments where there are no answers, please just be with me. I do not see yet how You can bring good from this, but I want to trust You like Jesus did.

APPLICATION

1. Close your eyes and imagine Jesus, pleading with the Father to take away the trial that was in front of Him. How does it feel to know that Jesus, as God Himself, wrestled with suffering?

2. All of us sometimes wish we could numb the pain with a temporary 'leprosy'. But in what ways does numbing pain open you up to more danger?

3. Have you seen someone else in your life 'suffer well'? What did that look like?

Time may close the gap
Smooth down the edges
But daggers cannot be undrawn
Fires unburned
Souls uncrushed

Tears, cleanse me now
A body too full of pain
Overflowing with bitter waters
Drenched in
Cold
Hard
Truth

# 4

TRAUMA

GETTING TO SAFETY

There are no words to express the confusion you endure when you realize that your best friend, your closest family, your lover has a whole life that you don't know about—a whole self that you have never seen. Everything in your heart and mind feels flipped on its head, and the disorientation is dizzying. Somehow, the person you knew the best is now a complete stranger.

It was hard for me to accept that my husband had become a stranger. It took time to fully comprehend that I actually did not know what he meant when he spoke, or how he really felt. *I did not know him.* It was even harder to accept that within him was something dark and malevolent. It wasn't just that he was a stranger now; there was a monster at work.

THE MONSTER WITHIN

I'll never forget the night the monster showed itself. It was several weeks after I caught him in the affair. He had returned to our home, and we were trying to reconcile. I had poured out my heart, *again*, about how much it hurt that he'd cheated, about how willing I was to forgive and repair this marriage, about how much I loved him. He seemed to listen, even to soften at times. It gave me hope.

Hope. What an enticing drug. When it's real, it's a powerful anesthetic, helping us endure a necessary surgery. But when it's false, it is a dangerous numbing that allows for another round of torture. If he could give me a little hope, even just an ounce, he knew I would stay.

But something in me was changing. He and I were used to me being whipped around by my intense emotions, yet that night, the Holy Spirit was at work, filling me with peace. There was no begging or desperation this time, just the truth. My spine strengthened into iron that couldn't be bent as I looked into his eyes with fierce love and honesty and power. He knew I wasn't messing around.

"I love you, but I don't need you. If you aren't going to choose me, clearly and fully, you will no longer have the choice to have me."

His eyes flashed with emotion: it wasn't fear of losing me, or shame for what he had done, or sorrow for breaking my heart. It was hatred. His eyes flashed with pure, unadulterated rage, as though I had violated *him*. He didn't speak, but I heard him loud and clear: I had threatened his grip. He didn't want to love me, but he didn't want to lose control of me.

My breath caught in my throat and adrenaline surged though my body. For the first time in our marriage, I chose to not be open and honest. I hid my heart. I pretended like I was fine, told him I needed to run an errand.

As soon as I closed the door to the house I collapsed to the ground. My whole body was shaking. I buried my head in my knees. "He doesn't care about you, he doesn't care about you, he doesn't care about you," I whispered repeatedly.

Some people might be surprised that after weeks of knowing of his affair this was a revelation to me, but it was. I had assumed he was lost, confused, enticed, and swept up. *But he still cared about me, right? He didn't mean to hurt me, right?*

Wrong.

There was a monster at work inside him. This was not him; it was something else, hidden inside of him. I could not unsee the ice in his eyes. It sent a chill right through me. That thing wished me harm—it hated me. That thing wanted me destroyed. It wasn't that we had grown apart, or just wanted different things out of life, or some other soft excuse. A dark spiritual battle was taking place inside of my husband. Something had been challenged by the supernatural strength and authority inside of me, and now it was exposed.

But the monster wasn't him. I just knew it couldn't be. There was a boy trapped in there, scared and tormented. There was a son of God, bound up in lies and oppression, but still carrying the fingerprint of our Father under all the darkness. I knew deep down he longed to be the man I wanted him to be, the man he really could be, a man of honesty and honor and courage. But that man was losing his fight to this demon, and I needed to get out of the way. The monster had control now and would demolish me if I let it. I didn't know how it got such a strong grip on him, or what it would take for him to conquer it from the inside out. What I did know was that allowing myself to be shattered wouldn't help him.

That night I determined in my heart to protect myself on a new level. My boundary lines had changed, and until that monster was gone for good, I was not going to be vulnerable with my husband. I was not hostile, and at that point I was still open to reconciliation, but I kept the deepest parts of me hidden. I began to change the locks to my heart, so he couldn't get in.

I knew I still loved him, at least that piece of him that was still there. If there was a tiny shred of the husband I had known, even if it was only a lie I had believed, my love for him was real. But I had to learn to reroute that love, because the monster thrived off it. It turned my love into a weapon against me, into my weakness. My love was not safe with him anymore—not while this monster was in charge.

So, I turned my love inward, holding it close. I didn't want the monster to see it, but decided to keep it safe for a time in case the monster inside of him was defeated. I changed the way I processed my thoughts and emotions, and instead of telling my husband how I was feeling, I wrote him letters that I never gave him. Whenever I was angry, lonely, missing him, or raging at him, I wrote a letter. I knew I could always share those letters with him if he really turned his heart back toward me and became safe for me again—but until then, I determined to wait.

Even as I held him at arm's length, I longed for him to become well enough that I could be close to him again. I wanted so badly for the man I loved to survive and take back his life, and I prayed continually for this to be possible. I prayed that he would rise up and fight back against this darkness, that he would cry out to the Lord and be filled with the Holy Spirit, who could cleanse and strengthen him. I believed in him, and in God's power to recreate him if he would just surrender to Jesus.

Ultimately, the monster in my husband was not defeated by him. There were glimmers of hope, but in the end, there was never true repentance, and my goodbye to him was permanent. I had to learn to live with the ghost of a man I once loved, a stranger walking around in his body. With time, I was able to have real compassion and kindness toward this stranger who was left in his place. But I needed space to get to that place, to accept the reality of what had happened to our marriage and who he had become, and to then heal and release what had been.

ACCEPTING REALITY

A common response in the body and the heart when a trauma has occurred is denial. When we have physical trauma, our body is designed to flood our brain with adrenaline and dopamine to minimize pain so that we can get to safety. In the same way, the shock and horror of an affair cannot be fully processed by our brains immediately. The initial rush of adrenaline is provided to get you to safety, but there is often confusion about where to run. The cruelest truth is that *your safest place*, your husband, *is the source* of the danger and the damage. There is such an intense disorientation with this, and it's common to have a period of denial at this stage.

This denial may not be what you think. You may not deny that this is happening. Whenever and however you found out about the affair is seared into your mind and heart. You will never forget that moment—I know I won't.

I remember with distilled clarity the night I found my husband in another woman's bedroom. The temperature of the air, the color of the door, the sound of my voice screaming, the shirt he was wearing, the look on his face . . . I knew what had happened, I knew what I saw. But I had a hard time accepting that he really understood what he was doing. I remember thinking, *This can't be right. He's a good guy. I know him. At least, I think I know him...* It took time for me to reconcile that he really was not a 'good guy'—that he knew what he was doing, and that the cost of his choices was a price he was willing to pay. That he was *choosing* this.

Dr. Clarke's book, "What To Do When He Says, I Don't Love You Anymore" opens with a startling and disturbing analogy that helped me to process this harsh truth. Imagine walking along the road and being shocked by the impact of a vehicle slamming into you. When you look, you see a familiar face in the driver's seat: your husband's. Dr. Clarke explains that while you may be shocked to see that your husband did this, you'd better get out of the way because he's about to run you over again. There was no misunderstanding, no mistake—your husband really knows that he is running you over. Your first job isn't to make sense of why. Your first job is to get out of the road. To get to safety. It is crucial that you move yourself out of harm's way as quickly as you can. Oftentimes that means putting up some boundaries to give you space and time to get your bearings.

A physical separation is not an overreaction to an affair. A woman needs space to grieve, receive support, and have time to be free from the confusion and triggers that come from relating to the adulterer.

The relational home of your marriage has been blasted, obliterated, and torn apart. The one place you thought you could turn is now a confusing mess of pain and mistrust, and it is likely that your husband has minimized or denied your anguish. The added disbelief from family, friends, or leaders, and the pressure to minimize or overlook the damage, may have left you feeling completely alone. But you deserve to have your experience validated; you deserve to get to safety so you can heal.

CHANGING THE LOCKS

I encourage you to give yourself permission to change the locks to your heart and get some emotional and physical distance for your safety. The space can help give perspective and clarity. It can be very difficult to tell the difference between the man you love and the dark stranger that seems to be steering his life. I know it may be completely against your nature to not trust your husband, but I urge you to let his actions speak to you. His words are unreliable, but his choices are loud, and they are enough to tell you what he wants and where he is going. He may be telling you that he loves you and that he is working on changing and that he deserves your trust and allegiance. If any of that is true, his *actions*, over a long span of time, will confirm it. Jesus teaches us in Matthew 7 to watch for fruit, and to judge actions:

> *Beware of false prophets who come disguised as harmless sheep but are really vicious wolves. You can identify them by their fruit, that is, by the way they act. Can you pick grapes from thornbushes, or figs from thistles? A good tree produces good fruit, and a bad tree produces bad fruit. A good tree can't produce bad fruit, and a bad tree can't produce good fruit. So every tree that does not produce good fruit is chopped down and thrown into the fire. Yes, just as you can identify a*

tree by its fruit, so you can identify people by their actions.

Matthew 7:15-20

If your husband really does love you and is truly sorry, he will allow you all the space and time you need to heal and will cooperate with what you ask of him in order to repair your marriage. If you feel resistance to any of that, beware of the darkness, and give yourself space and time to become grounded. It may be hard to accept, but you are likely not dealing with the man you think he is, or was, but with a dangerous stranger who has taken control. If he does not follow Jesus and respond to His voice, he is not a sheep, he is a wolf—and wolves are dangerous.

God does not expect you to continue to accept emotional, physical or sexual violence. You have permission to get to safety, in order to connect with Him and receive guidance on your next steps. In fact, it's imperative that you do. In the medical field, the first step with a trauma victim is to get them stabilized—that is your first task as well.

If you are dealing with physical intimidation and abuse or have any concern for your physical safety, please reach out to a professional resource in your area that has experience in assisting women who are victims of domestic abuse. I also recommend consulting with a lawyer to get recommendations for your situation. I have seen countless women not only be violated by the affair, but have their bank accounts emptied, their children put in unacceptable situations, and worse. I do not say this to scare you, but to awaken you to the reality that a man who is willing to violate your heart, body, and marriage is often willing to violate you in many other ways.

You might feel some guilt about treating a man you have loved like he is dangerous. After all, aren't we supposed to be forgiving and non-judgmental? Well, forgiveness, does not require reconciliation or proximity (although that is sometimes the outcome *after* repentance is established); it can happen from a distance. And while we are not qualified to judge someone's heart, or determine judgement on their soul, we are called to weigh their *actions* with the same measure we weigh our own (Matthew 7:1-3). Just as Jesus instructed His followers to examine fruit, we are exhorted by the Apostle Paul to judge sin inside of the church. He regularly supports godly shunning when a Christian is engaged in unrepentant sin, particularly sexual sin. One example of this is found in his letter to the church at Corinth:

> *But now I am writing to you not to associate with anyone who bears the name of brother if he is guilty of sexual immorality or greed, or is an idolater, reviler, drunkard, or swindler—***not even to eat with such a one***. For what have I to do with judging outsiders? Is it not those inside the church whom you are to judge? God judges those outside. "Purge the evil person from among you."*
>
> 1 Corinthians 5:11-13 (*ESV,* emphasis mine)

Paul's strong language is echoed all throughout Scripture (e.g., Matthew 18:15-17, 2 Thessalonians 3:14-15). God does not tolerate sin. His people are to remove themselves from those who are committing sin, for the *purpose* of bringing the sinner to repentance. Making sure that you are safe financially, physically, and legally does not eliminate the possibility of reconciliation. A truly repentant man will support and affirm your need to establish safety around you as you heal from this atrocious wound. A boundary to keep you safe is not a stumbling block for his repentance. In fact, a strong and firm boundary may be the most important thing you can do to make room for restoration.

Tolerating the sin enables it, but shunning serves two purposes: protection for the violated one and the rest of the church, and a wakeup call for the one bound in wickedness. Protecting yourself does not make it harder for your husband to repent, it actually creates a clearer opportunity for him to turn around.

Every woman's journey is unique, and your pathway to creating a safe space will likely look different than mine. Maybe you need to put your husband out of the house like I did or go stay with someone you trust. Perhaps you choose to not have that level of physical separation, but regardless of your situation, you do not need to apologize for getting to safety—not only does your heart need this space to heal, your body does also.

THE PHYSICAL IMPACT

Sometimes when there has been a relational trauma, we can forget that we experience our lives in bodily form. Emotional hurts and mental agonies are intrinsically linked to our physical selves. The parts in our brain where emotion is experienced and thoughts are formed are linked to how the rest of us functions. Our bodies cannot escape the consequences of the intensity, and it's important to care for your whole self, body included, as you cope and adjust.

Psalm 31 came alive to me in a new way, and I drew comfort from knowing that God's Word validated the distress I was experiencing. In the depths of his own despair, David wrote:

> *Have mercy on me, Lord, for I am in distress. Tears blur my eyes. My body and soul are withering away. I am dying from grief; my years are shortened by sadness. Sin has drained my strength; I am wasting away from within.*
>
> *Psalm 31:9-10*

The pain you are in is physical, just as it is emotional and mental. In this instance, your strength has been drained, not by your own sin, but by sin that was committed against you. You might experience a variety of discomforts and physical issues, from indigestion to irregular heart rhythms to muscle tension. You may even feel like you are physically dying—I know I felt that way. In the early days after the affair came to light, I couldn't eat. My stomach was a knot and refused food. Day after day my friends brought me meals, but I fed them to the kids. Or the toilet. I lost twenty pounds in a handful of weeks. You may gain weight, you may lose weight, but no one's body could go through this unscathed. It can feel like years are being scraped from your life. You are not being dramatic or overreacting. Your body is suffering from real and measurable distress.

Sleep can become a struggle, with your mind spinning and heart racing when your head hits the pillow and with nothing to distract you, you can be pulled into the ocean of pain and torment, thinking about what has happened. When you finally do fall asleep, the first few moments of waking might feel normal. There may be a few brief moments where you almost forget what happened. But forgetting is almost not worth it, because the nausea and adrenaline flood back like a tsunami when you remember. It's like all the horror and hurt gets held back, like a river dammed, only to rush in and flood you to make up for lost time.

Other times, sleep may not help you forget at all, and when exhaustion overtakes you and your body shuts down into sleep, you're tormented by nightmares. In my sleep, I would have unwelcome visions of their bodies coupled in sex, their laughter at me ripping through my ears. I would wake up in a sweat, weeping, screaming at nothing and no one. My body needed to rest, but it seemed like there was no escape from the panic and adrenaline. One woman I coached put it this way, "I wake up and I feel like I'm living in a nightmare, but it is my real life." This nightmare you are living is real, and it has a real impact on your body.

Our bodies carry trauma in different ways, and it's normal to have unexpected symptoms and need support medically. I reached out to my doctor to get medication and supplements to help with the nausea, anxiety, and sleeplessness. It's wise to connect with your doctor to create a specific plan about how to nurture and supplement what your body needs during this stressful season. You do not need to tough this out on your own.

It was helpful for me to view my body as my home and friend, whom I needed to survive the chaos. Your body is going through this difficulty with you, and you need each other. This season of your life won't last forever, and it's okay to need extra support during this time. Try not to feel embarrassed. If you'd been in a car accident and needed treatment, you would feel no shame. The kind of shock you've endured is sending so much cortisol and adrenaline through your body, that it's almost as though you're in a car accident every hour.

Your body was created by God to heal itself with time and support. Think of a cut on your finger. Your blood rushes to the scene to bring nutrients and infection fighting material. It begins to clot to eliminate further bleeding, and as it hardens to create a barrier against the outside, your body works to heal the cut from the inside out. All of this happens without you even thinking about it. But cleaning the wound, applying pressure, and using a bandage all help your body to do its work. In the same way, your body is designed to heal from this trauma on its own, but you can help it. Nourishing your body with good food, getting as much rest as you can, seeing a doctor, moving your body in whatever exercise you are able to do, and finding safe places to release emotion will help your body as it works to heal from the stress and suffering.

Getting distance from what is cutting you in the first place is also key. Reinjury prolongs the healing process and opens you up to more harm. Healing will take time, for both your body and your heart, but trust that God wants to lead you to a safe place so your healing can begin.

FINDING HOME

God created you for wholeness; He is angered by the violation of your marriage—and of your heart and body, and He is with you during this season of intense suffering. Whether your marriage survives or not is not His priority. *You are.*

The physical grief and stress that your body is enduring because of the affair is one of the most intense emotional and physical distresses ever experienced by humans. Your primary source of human connection has been disconnected. Your safest place is now dangerous. You are not overreacting; you are not crazy; you are in deep trauma.

In an interview with *Psychology Today*, Robert Stolorow said, "Trauma is when severe emotional pain cannot find a relational home in which it can be held."

The truth is, your pain needs a home.

Jesus wants to hold your pain. He wants to build and expand the place in your heart where you connect with Him so that you have a home inside of yourself in which this pain can be held; where His Holy Spirit can come alongside you to comfort and guide and heal your trauma. This is the longing of God: to create a place for you to come in this time when you are weary and burdened, a place where He can give you rest as Jesus says in Matthew 11:28.

At some point, I realized that if I took the pain from the affair and turned on myself or on God, I would be truly lost and permanently damaged. I had to create a deeper connection with Jesus to replace that inner space I had shared with my husband. Regardless of whether the relationship with my husband would ever be rebuilt, I needed a place to be protected while I coped with the damage. Of course, the support I found from family, friends, and professionals was invaluable, but staying connected with my own heart and with the Lord saved my life.

God won't force Himself on you—He allows us to choose. But once you have chosen Him, He will never leave you or forsake you. This is a promise He gives over and over in His Word (Deuteronomy 31:8, Hebrews 13:5). Whether you feel His nearness or not, you can trust it and believe in it. I urge you to press toward Him, to open your heart to Him. It is vital for your recovery that you cultivate safety within your relationship with yourself and with God. He is the only One who can give you the strength to unravel what has happened to you.

PRAYER

God, You know how wrecked I am by this trauma. You understand how my body, mind, heart, and spirit have been violated and wounded. Please give me wisdom to get to safety. Help me to resist the denial that tempts me to stay in harm's way. Give me courage to move, and to follow where You are guiding me. Thank You, Holy Spirit, that You are called my Comforter and Counselor. Create a home inside me, a safe space where You can hold my pain with me, comforting and guiding me. I need You desperately, and I trust that You are with me.

APPLICATION

1. How have your husband's actions created a danger for you—physically, emotionally, and mentally? Is it difficult for you to believe that your husband knows what he is doing? How is believing otherwise easier to accept?

2. In what space or relationship do you feel most safe?

3. What is your most troublesome physical symptom from the trauma? What is one way you can get help this week to take care of your body?

The darkness is thick
It presses down
Weighted in agony
Heavy in my lungs

Clouding the future
Suffocating the past

Was there beauty?
Is all lost?
Will I find home again?
What is real?

Shifting ground under my aching feet
Jolting and slick
I can't see it
But it punishes me

I stumble
Bruised and broken,
Brought to my knees
Again
Every second a terror

And yet

A light flickers through the fog
A strength rises in my breast

A warmth descends upon my head
An anointing, a holy call

My name is Faithful

I will walk on
Courage steadies me
Love lifts my head
Hope fills my chest

A Voice cuts through the silence

"You know who you are"

5

IDENTITY

REDISCOVERING WHO YOU ARE

Your world has crumbled. Your heart is shattered. Your worst nightmare is your daily reality, and you wake up each morning in disbelief that this is your life. The most sacred parts of your heart and your body have been desecrated. Violated. How can anyone heal from a wound this deep? A loss this severe?

After such a disorienting shock, it can be hard to know who you are anymore. In order to know how to move forward, you must find some semblance of who you really are.

I AM RUTH

I remember the first night after I found out my husband was cheating on me. With his words ringing in my ears, sleep was impossible. Over and over I heard, "I just don't love you anymore. I don't know if I ever loved you."

Was my whole marriage a lie? The possibility was unimaginable. It was too much. I couldn't breathe when that thought hit me. It seemed like the weight of all my reality hung on that question. *Do I know anything? Is anything steady? I lost him—do I have to lose everything else?* I reeled. My mind spun. I shook, as another wave of adrenaline surged through my body. Oh, my poor body. A hostage to grief;

the carrier of pain so deep my bones ached. But this anguish, this tingling of panic, was a sign that I was alive. I closed my eyes and breathed one more impossible breath.

My mind reached back for something solid. Something safe. Something real. It grabbed ahold of a moment when I was a young girl, experiencing the power and presence and love of God for the first time. My feet landed. I latched onto this memory tightly and looked at her face. This girl was me. She was whole. She was okay. This memory was rooted in the deepest place of my soul, and it was a bedrock of truth.

God is real.

His love is real.

I am real.

I began to whisper into my pillow, curled up in a fetal position, my whole body trembling, "I am Ruth. I am okay. I am Ruth. I am okay." I repeated this over and over, grounding myself in something outside of my marriage. Everything for the past ten years seemed like it was unsteady, so I focused on the knowledge that I existed before I knew my husband. That I was whole at the start. That my heart was mine. My breathing slowed; my body began to relax. *I am Ruth.*

Looking back, I see now how powerful that simple declaration was. The betrayal of an affair strikes at the root of a woman's identity causing us to question our worth and to ask, *Who am I now?* Beyond the shock and horror of seeing our husband in a new and terrifying light, we can also see ourselves differently. In an instant, our value is in question, and if we cannot separate our personal identity from our marital identity, we are at risk of being destroyed, as the marriage is destroyed. But if we can see that our souls, our real selves, exist outside of the relationship, we can survive, even as we suffer.

By acknowledging that I had an identity that the affair could not touch, I allowed God to protect the core of my heart, as the rest of it shattered to pieces. There was a part of myself that was being ripped apart—the married part of me. But I had to hold onto the part of me that existed before I had met my husband, and that would exist whether we fixed this or not, allowing God to define and protect my personal identity.

SEEING YOURSELF CLEARLY

We are built for community and connection. We all need relationships with others to reflect back to us who we are; this is what makes us human and helps us to know ourselves. Relationships are the mirrors in which we can start to see ourselves more clearly.

However, some mirrors are more reliable than others. Have you ever looked into a bent or broken mirror? The image is distorted. When I look into a mirror that is bent in a certain way, it can make me look like I gained or lost fifteen pounds. While the image is convincing, the truth is that I weigh the exact same no matter which reflection I see or prefer. I am who I am. That is reality. What I see reflected back to me and what is actually true, are sometimes quite different. In the same way, what our 'people-mirrors' reflect back to us can be distorted. We cannot fully rely on other people to show us who we are. We need the Perfect One to reveal our true identity; the Author of reality to tell us what is real.

Before we begin unpacking the affair's effects on your marital identity, we first must establish your core identity. Your heart is broken, and we must look at its original blueprint to put it back together again. *God created your heart.* He knows it inside and out— even better than you do—and His mirror is not bent or cracked. He is whole and complete, and never lies. He spoke life itself into existence and knows exactly who you are. He dreamed you up and crafted you with excitement, love, and tender care. You belong to God first, before anyone else. He created *you*—before your marriage. And now, He wants to speak your true identity over you again.

If you are struggling to hear His voice amidst the chaos of your questions, hold up the mirror of His Word.

> It says that you are fearfully and wonderfully made. His work in creating you is wonderful, and He wants you to know that full well (Psalm 139:14).
>
> You are chosen, by Him, before the creation of the world to be holy and blameless in His sight (Ephesians 1:4).
>
> You are being transformed into the image of the glory of the Lord; He is taking you from glory to glory and from strength to strength (2 Corinthians 3:18).
>
> You are upheld by His righteous right hand. There is no need to be afraid because He is with you. He is your God and He will strengthen and help you (Isaiah 41:10).
>
> You are redeemed. He calls you by name and you are His. So, fear not (Isaiah 43:1).

Scripture makes it clear that you are valuable, handcrafted, created in His image, and chosen by God. He is with you, for you, and calls you His own. It is stunning how much He loves and values you.

When we look to Him to define us, our identity can be established in an immovable, steady, objective way. Our feet can be firmly planted on solid ground because we have the truth to hold onto. But first, we have to ask ourselves if we believe Him, if we think He is qualified to define our worth. Most of us would not dare to say out loud that the Creator of heaven and earth is unworthy of deciding what is true about us, but let's be honest, we have all been tempted to question His authority on this subject. In small, subtle ways we believe the enemy's lies about ourselves instead of trusting what God has said. Just like Eve in the garden, our doubt in God's goodness leads to crisis and disconnection from our Maker and we find ourselves asking, *Did God really say that? Am I really loved? Is He really good?* We must consistently fight back against the enemy's lies and return to the only One who has the right to tell us who we are.

There is an unshakeable truth about you: You are loved. You are valuable. This is what God says about you, as His daughter, all throughout Scripture. Your true worth is not in question unless you do not believe God. So, it boils down to this: What do you believe? Is God trustworthy, or is He a liar? Your feelings will waver, but you get to decide what you believe. If you allow God to define you and keep returning to His truth when you encounter waves of insecurity and shame, He will hold your identity together.

Conversely, when we allow other people to define us, our identity can only be understood in a fragile, unsteady, subjective way. If your husband gets to decide your worth, your value is always at risk. You are only loved if someone chooses to love you, you are only worthy if someone else says so, you only hold the value someone else assigns. Even in a healthy marriage, that kind of power was never meant to rest in another human's hands. You were not created for this kind of instability.

Truth is either objective, or it's not truth at all. So, if God does not lie, and He says you are loved and worthy and chosen, *that* is who you are, and it cannot change. No rejection, mistreatment, or lie from hell can undo what God says. The voice that spoke all of creation into being has spoken that *you are loved*. Believe me, God is more qualified to define who you are than this man who has wounded you, or this circumstance that is out of your control.

Women whose husbands are unfaithful to them have often been looking into a distorted mirror for quite some time. Typically, men who have affairs are quite skilled at lying and manipulating. Your husband has deceived himself, and has tried to deceive you. He is obviously not listening to God right now, and probably has been walking in disobedience for a while. It's likely that you have believed lies about yourself for much longer than the affair has been going on. Many women are so beaten down inside by the time the affair comes to light that they don't even know who they are anymore. It causes such deep confusion to have your reality reflected back to you with so much distortion, that many women stop trusting themselves long before they stop trusting their husbands. Or, perhaps you did not believe his reflection of you, but you have been trying to convince him to see who you really are. The tension that creates is exhausting, perplexing, and frustrating.

Your husband is a broken mirror. While he is engaging in an affair, you should not believe a single word he says. He is in deep deception, so expect lies from him. I am not saying that to demean him, but to honor the reality of the path he has chosen. Do not look to him to see yourself clearly. The enemy has attacked your personal identity through your husband's actions and the shattered mirrors are calling your name. You may have been looking into distorted glass for years, believing lies about what you were seeing. You must now learn to look to the God who created you. Let Him define your personal identity. Trust Him. Believe Him.

Believing God is not a one-time choice; it is a life-long discipline, an exercising of your trust muscle. In this season where your life has been turned upside down, you will need to return to this over and over. As you practice exchanging lies about yourself for truth, exchanging the broken mirror for the perfect one, you will get stronger. With time and repetition, your self-concept will solidify—keep turning your eyes to Jesus.

As I walked through my fire, I had to constantly replace lies about my identity with the truth in Scripture. When I would think, *I am unloved*, I would remind myself that the God of the universe loves me and that nothing can separate me from that love (Romans 8:35). When I thought, *I am worthless*, I reminded myself that I was redeemed with the highest price imaginable, Jesus' blood (1 Peter 1:19). When I felt alone, I reminded myself that God was with me, and would *never* leave (Isaiah 43:2, Matthew 28:20). When

I felt rejected, I remembered that I was chosen by God Himself (Ephesians 1:4). When I felt like a total failure, I chose to believe that in Christ, I was more than a conqueror (Romans 8:37). When I felt like I had no hope, I decided to trust that Christ within me was the hope of glory (Colossians 1:27). I pasted God's Word on my bathroom mirror, in my car, on my fridge, at my kitchen sink. I had to constantly wash my mind with Scripture to combat the attacks on my identity, and as I did, God fought for me and with me. He protected the core of who I am from the damage this disaster was trying to inflict on me. And He will do the same for you.

When you find yourself slipping into despair over who you are and what this affair says about you, ask yourself what mirror you are looking into. Evaluate whether you are believing God's truth or the lies of the enemy, and remind yourself of who you truly are. Declare over your life, "I am a daughter of the Most High King. My value is secure in Jesus. *I am loved.*"

YOUR MARRIAGE IS NOT YOU

Once you have more clarity on your personal identity, you are in a stronger place from which to address your marital identity, which is what is at stake here. Remember, your marriage is hugely important and valuable, but your marriage is not you. It defines a large portion of your life, but it does not define you. Only God has the right to do that.

As I understood the difference between my marriage and myself, I could see the truth. I realized:

My husband does not love me, but *I am loved by God.*

My husband does not value me, but *I am valued by God.*

My husband is not trustworthy, but *I can trust God.*

My husband is lying to me, but *God will always speak the truth to me.*

My marriage is dead (or at least dying), but *I am alive.*

My identity as a wife was completely shattered by my husband's affair, but my personal identity as God's daughter was not. Although my marriage was mortally wounded, and I did not know if it could live again or if we could heal together, I trusted that God had life for me, that He was going to heal me—with or without my husband.

Do not get me wrong, there were many, many dark moments where I believed my life was over and I thought I might actually die from the pain. It was hard for me to see where the edge of the marriage was and where I began—we were one flesh, and I felt ripped apart when he betrayed me. It seemed as though everything was lost. But those moments did not last, and I continued to find my feet planted on the firm rock of God's Word. Slowly, surely, I began to see the space between my marriage and my *self*.

As I held the bleeding body of my marriage, this space was critical to my survival. There were times where it became hard to discern if the blood was mine or the marriage's; I was covered in it. It was so important for me to understand that while I could not stop my husband from killing the marriage, *I could stop the enemy from destroying me*. If I had allowed the lies and the evil that destroyed my marriage to get into my heart, it very well could have been my blood spilling out as well. By the grace of God, I was able to separate myself from the marriage, and walk into new life even though my marriage could not.

Regardless of whether your marriage survives or not, it is imperative that *you* survive, sister. Not only physically, but emotionally and spiritually as well. You must fight for yourself. I know you are tired and confused—that you feel broken. But there is an instinct to *live* inside of you. You were created to overcome. You can make it through this.

Separating and prioritizing your personal identity does not mean your marital identity is un-important. It is a huge part of who you are and the pain you are feeling over its devastation is real and deep. Remember, God designed you. He honors the choice you made to be married, and values that part of your heart. There is a reason that this death blow to your marriage hurts you so profoundly—you are connected to your marriage. There is an exchange of life between you and it, and it cannot exist without you. You have drawn strength, love, and identity from it, as you were designed to do.

But the truth that looms large is this: Your marriage is being destroyed by the one person who promised you they would protect it. This attack on your marital identity is not coming from outside of your union, but from the inside. The reason your husband has the power to do so much damage to the marriage is because of his position within it. This place of connection, this sacred union between you and him, is a place that he has had rightful access to, and he has abused that right.

In a healthy marriage, a husband can and should speak truth about his wife's identity. A man's strength and influence should be used to serve, protect, and promote his wife. No one does this perfectly, of course, but the mirror of a husband, the closest one possible, should be one that you can trust. *Should*.

This is why such abuse can happen when a spouse turns. The access into your life is fully open. You have trusted deeply, as any spouse should, and the road into your heart is wide. It should allow love, truth, and safety in. Instead, it is being used to traffic lies, curses, and destruction. What was meant to be a river of life into your soul has been poisoned into a river of death.

Your identity as a wife has been violated and demolished. The vows promised to you have been broken. No doubt you feel shaken to your core about who you are as a wife. That part of you has been turned upside down and there is no denying the huge sea of unknowns in front of you. But your worth and value can be known; your personal identity can be protected and rooted in a safe place. When everything else has been thrown into chaos, hold onto your heart. When everything about your marriage is brought into question, be confident in Who defines you. Feel your feet on the floor. Take another deep breath with your lungs. In this moment, know who you are and Whose you are.

UNDERSTANDING THE BETRAYAL

Now that we have established your personal identity in Christ, and how it is connected to, but separate from your marital identity, we can unpack how to understand the betrayal you have experienced. As tempting as it is to believe that the rejection is telling you something about *you*, it is actually telling you something about *him*.

We will continue to come back to this truth: *You cannot control someone else*. We all understand this on some level, but I know well the taunting questions your heart will be wrestling with. *Was this my fault? Could I have stopped this? What did I do to make him turn away?*

Every woman I have coached has felt pummeled by those questions, and many have blamed themselves. But sister, if we were together right now, could you look in my eyes and tell me my husband's affair was *my* fault? I doubt it. Please zoom out with me, try to be objective, hard as it may be. You did not make this choice, he did.

Yes, you know all your imperfections, and all the ways you've failed. Lord knows I had a laundry list of things that I had done wrong too, and it was okay for me to own those. Repent to the Lord if you need to. But know that nothing you have done is big enough or bad enough to control someone else's choices. *You are not that powerful*. We are each responsible for our choices, and our choices alone. If you were causing your husband so much trouble and hurt that it merited ending the relationship, he could have ended the relationship. But that's not the choice he made. He chose to have an affair. *He* chose that. It is not your fault.

Ask yourself, if you take responsibility for his choices, *shouldn't you be able to change them?*

The reason you are tempted to take responsibility is because you want to take control. I understand that. You are being violated and pulverized and you want it to stop. You want to make him stop. But you can't. That's not how life works, that's not how love works. The only love you can control is the love you give. That love reflects what you are made of because it comes from inside of you. It is yours. If someone else won't love you in return, that reflects on what is coming from inside of them, not you.

Your husband's rejection of you is saying some things loud and clear about *him*. It tells you what he values, what he believes, who he is following. The rejection does not tell you about your worth or value. Remember, God has already spoken on that, and it is not up for debate. No matter if you have made huge mistakes or if you have been the most amazing wife ever, your good or bad behavior does not control your husband's choices.

Consider Jesus with me. He is perfect. He made absolutely no mistakes while He walked this earth. He loved and lived flawlessly. Now picture Him washing His disciples' feet, speaking truth over them, giving them every opportunity to choose Him. They all experienced perfect love from Jesus, yet they each had the freedom to decide if they would love Him in return. John chose to love Him faithfully, remaining with Him at the cross (John 19:26-27). Peter denied Him three times (Matthew 26:33-35; 69-75), yet repented and was restored in relationship with Jesus, becoming a bold leader in the church (John 21). And Judas betrayed Jesus and did not return to Him, but took his own life after selling Him out for thirty coins of silver (Matthew 27:1-10). These three had very different responses to the *same* Messiah. The choices did not reflect on Jesus' worth, but on the hearts of each man. Even now, two millennia later, we are all given the freedom to choose to surrender to His perfect love or refuse Him. If Jesus Himself can be rejected, as perfect as He is, it is clear that even the purest love cannot force another into returning love.

I realized that my husband was rejecting *God Himself*, as well as me. If Jesus was not good enough for Him, how could I expect to be? It started to become clear to me that his choices were not a measuring stick for my worth, or a barometer of how well I loved him, but were simply the outpouring of what was in his heart. As Jesus taught, "A good person produces good things from the treasury of a good heart, and an evil person produces evil things from the treasury of an evil heart" (Luke 6:45).

The adultery revealed a deep root of evil that had been allowed to grow in my husband's heart. I could no longer deny what the rejection was telling me: My husband was lost and in desperate need of repentance. My prayers changed from, "Make me good enough to win him back," to "Protect me and deliver him from this evil." Rather than trying to change my husband's choices, I focused on listening to what they were telling me about who he was choosing to become.

No matter what your husband decides to do, remember to plant yourself deep into the soil of God's truth. Hold fast to the unshakable truth that you are loved by Him, and your identity is secure as His daughter, come what may. Once you know who you are, you are positioned to fight for what God has for your future.

PRAYER

God, thank You for being the true source of my identity. Even when it is hard to believe, I know the way You see me is more secure and safe than any other. Help me look to You when I am lost and confused, rather than to my husband. I want Your love and truth to define me, not my feelings or the lies that I have believed. Protect my heart and mind from distorted mirrors and show me the truth, as You hold me close.

APPLICATION

1. Write out your name. Say it out loud, "I AM _____." Now, close your eyes and travel back to a time untouched by this trauma. Where you were safe, and you were whole. That is who you are, even now. Describe the girl / woman you see.

2. What are three things that are true about you, based on what God says about you?

3. Armed with the truth that you cannot control your husband's choices, what is his rejection of you telling you about *him*?

Here we go again—
Betrayed by that heart on your sleeve
So exposed it bleeds

All it takes is a song
A reminder of the trust
So completely raw
So simple and sweet

Just one line and you are back

That first night
Naked again
For just his eyes to see

"I will never leave"
Such simple words
Cheap and clean
As lies tend to be

You can know it's not your fault
But the Pain . . .
It grips
And it shakes
And it drains
And it wins
And you die
Then you live

But you are still alone
The old is no more
The new is not yet
So you cry and wail and pound your chest

All you had was
All you gave and
All was thrown away
So far away

Where is it?
Where is the love you spent?
Is it locked inside him,
Buried treasure for a rainy day?

You will never know
It is yours no longer
It was a gift
Let it be

You were not a fool, dear,
You were a lover
Brave and tender
Handing over that heart

But it is yours again so keep it safe
Right there on that sleeve
For the beautiful world to see

6

LIES

FIGHTING BACK WITH TRUTH

Uncovering an affair causes us to question everything. Nothing seems certain anymore and we find ourselves wondering, *What do I really know?* You know that you've been lied to, but not how long it's been happening. You know that it wasn't always like this, but you're not sure if you can trust anything he's ever said or done. There's a mix of truth and lies, and it takes time to sift through the shattered glass of your life. I spent hours poring through phone records and credit card statements, piecing together the timeline. Unearthing the affair turned me into a manic detective. It was maddening, but I needed to create some sort of narrative to make sense of what had happened. You may also feel like there are some things you just need to know in order to be able to move forward. You can't go to the source to get the truth, because he has lied about so much. So, what *can* you know?

There are some universal truths in these situations, even though the specific details in your life and your marriage are unique. There are also some universal lies. The same excuses and reasonings from adulterers have been used for years: *I don't love you anymore. We've grown apart. I never loved you. I felt pressured to marry you. I feel trapped. I need space. I need to find myself. I love you but I'm not in love with you.*

As I heard other women's stories about their husband's infidelity and read books on the subject, I was astonished at how the same lies and defenses were echoed over and over again. These are common lines, common lies. It was both sickening and yet encouraging to know that there was some pattern of predictability in my husband's behavior. It's like the enemy has a script, and my husband was just mindlessly reading off every line. He seemed to really believe these lies. He had become so deceived that he created a false reality to justify his sin.

The enemy of our souls is not creative. He is persistent, but his tricks are as predictable as they are malevolent. The attack plan that he used on your spouse was not original. As wise Solomon says in Ecclesiastes 1:9, "There is nothing new under the sun" (ESV).

Conversely, the plan of attack the enemy has for you is also a replica. We are going to walk through some of the lies that the enemy frequently uses to injure women who are victims of affairs. It's likely that you have already battled against them, and you are not alone. Every woman that I have coached and walked alongside on this dark road has encountered these same untruths. How you respond to these lies will impact your healing greatly. The most powerful thing you can do is refuse to believe the lying tongue of the enemy. He has deceived your spouse, but he cannot deceive you without your permission. Do not be ashamed if you've already believed these falsehoods—it's never too late to turn toward the truth.

"If I can change, he will stop."

It is tempting to think that you can control something to make this pain stop. The thoughts come in: *Maybe if I lose some weight. Maybe if I don't get so emotional when we argue. Maybe if I never nag again about the bills … the kids … the in-laws … Maybe I can fix it.*

Maybe if you're more amazing and lovable he will have *no choice* but to come back to you, right? Maybe if you are perfect, then he will *have to* love you. Pay attention to that language, sister.

Have to. Must. No choice.

This is not the language of love. This is the language of control, and it is a lie. It isn't really what you want, if you are honest with yourself. You don't want to force him to love you. You don't want to make him want you. What you want is to be chosen—freely, permanently. Nor do you want to have to perform for love, to earn it, or pull it out of someone. You want to be loved in sickness and in health, for richer or for poorer, for better or for worse. That is what you were promised. I'm fairly confident that your husband's vows to you didn't say that he would forsake all others only as long as he felt like it. As long as you behaved. As long as you were perfect. You didn't agree to that on your wedding day. Don't agree to it now.

Our culture is saturated in the lie that love is a byproduct of compatibility, or destiny, or chemistry. The world is addicted to ease, and it has created a trapdoor for marriage. If it's not easy, it must not be right. The enemy's lie is that if your husband doesn't want to do the hard work of choosing love, he can put the blame on you. Your husband may have bought into that lie, but you don't have to. The truth is that love is a choice. Love requires sustained effort, effort that your husband promised to make. He is responsible for fulfilling his vows.

He can change, and he can stop.

He has the ability to end the affair, turn away from sin, repent fully and completely, and enter into a serious recovery period where he takes full responsibility. I have seen that happen. It is possible.

During the first months of my separation from my husband, I reached out to a number of women whose husbands had been unfaithful. About half of them had healed together, with their marriages reconciled. The other half had healed alone, after divorce. I admired all these women and saw hope and wholeness in each one's life. I asked them so many questions, trying to uncover the common thread: *What makes a man stop cheating? What did these women do, whose husbands repented, that the other women did not do?*

The Lord stopped me in my tracks. It was not about what these women did. It was the *men* in those marriages who decided the outcome.

All the women I was looking to did the same thing—they surrendered their shattered hearts to Jesus. They were promised His love and His healing, regardless of the marriage's survival. The men that repented in time and fully owned their sin made it possible for reconciliation to happen; the men who continued to walk in sin were responsible for the divorces. It was that simple.

Your husband can change. If he does, it's because he chooses to. If he doesn't, it is because he doesn't want to.

Part of me wanted to assume the blame for my husband's affair, so I could take control and make the change. But as I faced the truth over and over that I could not change anyone but myself, I had to accept the lack of control. It was a relief, and it was terrifying. Things seemed out of control because they actually were. In reality, I had never had control of my husband, and I never would. I was not designed to control anyone else.

It was crucial for me to see who was behind the lie that the affair was somehow my fault—that the enemy wanted to burden me with something I was powerless over, destroying my hope. I had to determine in my heart to not let this thief and liar guide how I thought or how I defined myself. God was the only One worthy to define me, and He was clear in Scripture that He placed the burden of fault for the affair squarely on the shoulders of my husband.

"He doesn't mean to hurt me. He can't help himself."

I know that your husband is probably not doing this *just* to hurt you. However, he is absolutely willing to do this knowing full well that it *does* hurt you. He did not care enough about you to choose otherwise. No one is ignorant enough to think that engaging in an extramarital affair, whether physical or emotional, would not hurt their spouse. Everyone knows that it will. He knows this hurts you, and he is doing it anyway. He is a grown man, and he is doing what he wants to do.

Unrepentant adultery is abuse. It is an act of hatred. I know those are strong words, but I will not make excuses for this emotionally violent act that has been made against you. God Himself calls it violence in His Word when the prophet Malachi warns His people about how their infidelity has broken marriage covenants:

> *"The man who hates and divorces his wife," says the LORD, the God of Israel, "**does violence to the one he should protect**," says the LORD Almighty. "So be on your guard, and do not be unfaithful."*
>
> *Malachi 2:16 (NIV, emphasis mine)*

It is especially important, if your husband has seen how his actions have affected you and still has not taken responsibility and stopped, for you to accept how little he cares. Tears, excuses, promises all mean nothing; His actions will tell you what you need to know.

He does mean to hurt you. He can help himself.

I understand firsthand how tempting it is to make excuses for him, rather than accept the cold, hard truth. I thought if I could blame my husband's choices on some psychotic break, or some larger reality that was *making* him do this—a world where he had no choice—it would make it easier for me. I was still in denial for a time. But as I began to accept that he was choosing this, fully capable of changing, I realized that it was actually *more* honoring of him as a human for me to acknowledge his responsibility for his choices. To suggest that he was a helpless victim to this evil implied that he was weak and like a child, when in reality he was a strong man. Unfortunately, he was using his strength and his choices to hurt me. That is abuse, dear one. That is the only word for it.

Infidelity is not a mistake. It is a choice. It is sin. A mistake is backing the car into the garage door, or forgetting to take the garbage out. The affair did not happen accidentally, or innocently. Your husband did not forget that he was married to you, or what his vows were. Sin hardens hearts, and makes people blind, but adultery is not an honest mistake.

At some point, your husband had a choice to start down this path. I am guessing that there was a part of him that wanted to do the right thing and turn away from the temptation. However, he didn't fight hard enough. He allowed himself to succumb to a mindset that excused his choices. Now, he has taken step after step, engaging in sin after sin, lie after lie, and he has dug himself into a hole that will be very difficult to exit. It will not save him if you fall into the pit with him. If anything, it's more helpful for you to stay on solid ground and offer a right perspective, even if it means hard boundaries or a goodbye. Do not enable the lie. It won't help him, and it certainly will not help you.

"He is happy with her."

It is easy to look at the couple having the affair and believe that they are happy. I remember finding receipts for hotels, restaurants, and gifts that my husband had gotten his paramour. They were partying it up while I was at home making mac and cheese with my kids on a shoestring budget. While I was nursing the baby in the middle of the night, he was wrapped up with another woman's body. I had noticed how he lit up around her before I knew about the affair and realized that it had been years since I had had that effect on him.

You may have noticed similar trends. Maybe he is dressing up more than usual, wearing a new cologne, working out more, acting like he has finally found himself. Maybe he tells you that he loves her in a way that he just never loved you. So, is he happy?

He is not happy.

He is intoxicated. He is delirious. He is drugged. But he is not truly happy in any meaningful sense. Remember, God is the One who designed our hearts and bodies for connection. His way is always good for us, and this affair is way outside of what is good. This affair is evil. It is bad. Not only is this toxic for you, but it is toxic for your husband and his mistress. God is clear in Scripture about what is underneath the facade, and where the path of adultery leads:

> *He who commits adultery lacks sense; he who does it destroys himself. He will get wounds and dishonor, and his disgrace will not be wiped away.*
>
> *Proverbs 6:32-33 (ESV)*

These are strong words. Your husband is *destroying* himself. He *will* get wounds and dishonor. This is not what may happen, it is what will happen. These are sure truths in God's Word. Your husband has not chosen a pathway to happiness; he is walking into destruction and darkness. I encourage you to trust what God says over what you feel in these moments of jealousy and comparison. I know how difficult that can be, but God has a perspective above ours and He does not lie. True joy can only be found in God's presence and following in His way. Your husband is not following God and is in darkness. There may be fleeting pleasure there, but there is no true joy.

"I should have seen this coming."

As our minds try to make sense of the chaos of our new reality, it can be easy to blame ourselves for not sensing that something was off earlier than we did. We may think that if we had been more perceptive, we could have changed things, or protected our hearts from the hurt. But the truth is that no one can see the future, and no one can predict someone else's choices. You did not know what you did not know.

You could not have seen this coming.

The problem with hindsight is that no one has it in time. No one gets married thinking their spouse would cheat on them. Love is built on trust, and just because your husband *became* untrustworthy does not mean your initial trust was in error. You loved and respected your spouse and believed the best in him for as long as you could. That is admirable. Rather than beating yourself up for not suspecting the affair earlier than you did, try to honor the trust that you invested.

At any time prior to the affair, my husband could have made different choices, and ended up in a completely different place in our marriage. Not only could I not anticipate his choices, I had no control over them. Neither did you.

Like most women in this situation, I never knew anything other than this marriage. Especially if this was your first marriage, it's common for you to have thought every dynamic and struggle was normal—many of them truly were. For those that were not, perspective or foreknowledge would not have given you the power to change his behavior. Your husband is not a programmable robot, he is a human with free will. No person could have foreseen his affair. He was not destined to do this, he chose to.

"She has something that I don't."

It would be painful enough to be rejected by your husband, but it adds insult to injury that he didn't just leave, he chose another woman. A woman with a body, with a personality, with a story. Or perhaps he chose a man, or a prostitute, or a child who could not say no. Regardless of the nature of his infidelity, insecurity will try to convince you that you lack something that he found in someone else.

When I realized that my husband wasn't just drifting away from me emotionally, but that he was in love with someone else, waves of self-doubt overwhelmed me. *Is she better in bed? Does she always have the right thing to say? I bet she doesn't have morning breath like me or have these stretch marks I carry from his babies. She must have everything that I lack. Why else would he walk away from a beautiful life, a strong community, innocent children, a fiercely loyal wife? He knew how much I loved him. What makes losing all of this worth it to him? It must be her, right?*

In my case, I knew this woman. We were friends, and we worked together. I liked her. I thought she was pretty and funny. Once I found out they were together, my insecurities highlighted the ways I thought she was better than me. She was thinner and hadn't carried babies—I bet she wore black lacy bras, while I wore faded nursing bras with milk-stained pads. I was certain she showered more often than I did. After being up all night with the kids, it was a miracle to just wear actual pants, and my hair always found itself in a messy bun. I had always been a scaredy-cat, not even riding my bicycle very fast, whereas she was edgy and rode a motorcycle. Maybe she was sexy and cool in a way I never could be. Maybe the bad-girl vibes satisfied him more than my pure love could. I thought I was what he wanted—that is what he told me—but obviously I was not. These thoughts left me feeling caved in. I felt like I was back in a middle school dance—sweaty, small, and out of place.

Other times, my pride highlighted the ways I thought I was better. It was so tempting to judge her with disgust, as someone far beneath me. Picking her apart helped mask some of my insecurity, but it never lasted. Even if I felt superior for a few moments, the truth was that my husband was choosing her, not me. The slimy, dirty residue from judging her didn't help. It just made me feel guilty and further away from God.

Once again, I had to ask the One who knows so much more than I ever could for answers. The only One who really knows my heart, who really knows her heart. It was excruciating, but I asked God to show me how He saw this woman. What He showed me changed everything.

She has a broken life that is beneath her dignity.

I saw her as a little girl, shivering in the fetal position, dirty and hiding in rags. She was beautiful, but she was covered in scars from men using and hurting her. I may never know her full story, but I felt God's heart breaking for her. The depth of pain that causes a woman to engage in an affair, to accept such a pitiful offering from a man, is staggering. Her heart longed for love, but she was accepting cheap lust. She was designed for permanence, but she was chasing a fling. She was created to build a family of her own, but she was destroying someone else's instead. She was lost, blind, and lonely. She had no idea how much God loved her. I couldn't help but have pity on her.

Most men who are willing to cheat, are also willing to lie to their new partner. Your husband may have told his mistress that he was already divorced, or that the marriage was headed that direction. He is also likely to lie *about* his mistress, and tell you he's been seduced, tricked, etc. You likely won't ever know what the truth is, but the main betrayal is from him, not her.

The idea that the other woman has something that you lack is a lie. The truth is that what you lack is a faithful husband. That is not your fault, and really, it is not her fault either. She couldn't make him cheat any more than you can make him stay true to you. She is responsible for her choices, and they are inexcusable. She knows it, and she will suffer for it. But she doesn't have a faithful husband either. She has the leftovers of a man who is willing to lie, steal, hide, blame, and hurt a woman that he promised to love. This is not a great prize, and while your jealousy over your husband is completely justified, what she has is not enviable.

"My sexuality is ruined."

I remember feeling like damaged goods. I was humiliated to have to get a sexually transmitted infection test after the affair came to light. I had only ever been with one man, who I was married to. As I lay on that bed getting tested, legs spread, tears streaming down my face, my body felt violated and dirty. How could I ever trust someone to touch me again? Who would want me?

You may feel like this violation to your body has changed everything, that it defines your sexuality permanently. However, while someone else's choices *affect* you, they do not define you. Remember, only God has the authority to define you, and He says that you are fearfully and wonderfully made. While you might feel otherwise right now, He is in the business of making new creation, of making broken things whole, of making dead things come alive. He can, and will, redeem anything that you put in His hands.

Your sexuality can be restored.

By His grace, God has literally wiped away memories, old heart ties, and every residue of my sexual wounds. God wants to do that in your life too. There is nothing you can do in your own strength to remake yourself, but God has the power to heal every part of you. In Jeremiah 30 He declares, "But I will restore you to health and heal your wounds" (v.17, NIV).

We often misunderstand sexuality, elevating it to a place it was never designed to be. Sex does not determine your value; it is an act of sharing the value you already have. Sex is about showing and giving yourself and seeing and receiving someone else. As you allow God to remind you of the truth about who you are, who you have been since before you met this man, and the intrinsic worth God created you with, you will be able to share that again, not out of desperation, revenge, or need, but out of a beautiful generosity of self. You can be free again inside the safety of knowing you are treasured by God and designed to share pleasure inside a secure covenant. You are not there now, but only because that safe and sacred space has been violated. There is nothing wrong with your sexuality, there is something wrong with the situation. You are not broken; the covenant is broken. Unless and until you are cherished and protected within a real marriage, safeguard your body. Do not settle for anything less than sexual connection inside a healthy covenant relationship—that is what you deserve.

It is also helpful to remember that ultimately the infidelity is a *rejection of God*, not you. I know it may not feel that way, but someone else's sexual choices do not reflect your worth or value, but rather their own character. The Apostle Paul explains this:

> *It is God's will that you should be sanctified: that you should avoid sexual immorality; that each of you should learn to control your own body in a way that is holy and honorable, not in passionate lust like the pagans, who do not know God; and that in this matter no one should wrong or take advantage of a brother or sister. The Lord will punish all those who commit such sins, as we told you and warned you before. For God did not call us to be impure, but to live a holy life. Therefore,* **anyone who rejects this instruction does not reject a human being but God,** *the very God who gives you his Holy Spirit.*
>
> 1 Thessalonians 4:3-8 (NIV, emphasis mine)

When your husband rejected God's template for sexuality, he primarily rejected Him, not you. While you have been wronged and taken advantage of, God promises to vindicate you.

You are only responsible for your own choices. Be careful during this time to not fall into the same trap of sexual disobedience to God, in reaction to your hurt. The key to sexual health and identity is always surrender to Jesus and His ways. He created us. He designed us. He knows what is best for us, what will hurt us, and how to heal us. Somehow, He has the ability to walk us through these fires and keep us from being consumed. He is with you, and for you. Stay near to Him, trust Him with your brokenness, and watch Him make you whole again.

"I was stupid for loving and believing him."

Finding out that my husband had a whole secret life made me feel so foolish. How did I fall for so many lies? Was I some gullible idiot? I felt embarrassed, ashamed—like I had been showing up to our marriage totally naked. Stripped bare physically, emotionally, spiritually, he had gotten to see everything. I was fully exposed to him, and nothing was hidden. For years, I thought he was showing up like that too. I thought we were both vulnerable, both naked. Turns out, he was fully clothed, and I felt like a fool.

After some time and perspective, I began to rethink it. What is marriage? It is vulnerability, exposure, nakedness, *together*. I began to look back on my vulnerability as courage, not stupidity. I did my part. That was the right thing to do, the beautiful thing to do. I believed in him. That was also the right thing to do, the beautiful thing to do.

You were not stupid for loving and believing him.

Loving him and believing him were exactly what you promised to do on your wedding day. Your commitment and grace and trust are not signs of weakness; they are signs of strength and health. You were obedient to the Lord. Showing up for your marriage, leaning into it, choosing to love with an open heart—these are things to be proud of. That is the kind of love you were created to give. You were also created to receive it, and *that* is where the breakdown happened. There was nothing wrong with the amount of love and trust you gave. It was a beautiful gift that you offered inside the safety of covenant. The fact that the covenant has now been broken does not negate the value of the gift. You can hold your head up high, knowing that your love was real.

You may have had some red flags, or suspicions. Looking back on the lifespan of my marriage, there were certainly things that were unhealthy. But just because something is unhealthy does not mean that it must stay that way, or that it is not worth it to keep trying to improve. Remember the analogy of the marriage as a child. When my child gets sick, I do not give up on them and schedule an appointment for them to be euthanized. No, I do all I can to nurse them back to health. It was right for me to try to work through difficulties in my marriage, and it was right for you to do the same. You were not stupid, you were faithful. Your husband was unfaithful, and that is not your fault.

The lies we explored here, and others, are designed to take advantage of your hurt and vulnerability. I encourage you to seek God daily and invite Him into your thoughts. He will help you battle in this war on your mind and beliefs. Do not be afraid; lies disintegrate under the weight of God's truth. His Holy Spirit will empower you to "demolish arguments and every pretension that sets itself up against the knowledge of God, and . . . take captive every thought to make it obedient to Christ" (2 Corinthians 10:5, NIV). Capture your thoughts, make them obedient to Jesus, and you will walk in the freedom and healing you were made for.

PRAYER

God, thank You for Your truth. Help me to see it, receive it, and believe it. Guard me from the lies of the enemy. Give me strength to fight back against the darkness, and to cling to the light. You are worth believing. I commit to capturing my thoughts and making them obedient to Christ. I praise You that Your truth is always better and stronger than any lie I face.

APPLICATION

1. As you reflect on the lies I have identified, which has been most tempting for you to believe? Why do you think that is?

2. Pick whichever truths felt powerful for you to read, and write them out on a sticky note for your mirror or some place that you can see regularly to remind yourself of the truth.

3. Pray and ask God to reveal if there are any other lies you are believing that are not listed. See if you can hear God telling you the truth. If you get stuck, ask a trusted friend for their perspective.

Waking . . .
Remembering, all at once
The pain dulls with time,
But in sleep
My heart can forget
The knife twists
Again
Circles, jagged and raw

Rising . . .
Brave, determined, free
My life
My home
My path
The Thief stole him, but not me
I am here
Living and growing

Moving . . .
Coffee, daily readers, rhythm
Apple juice in sippy cups
Tousled hair
Rosy-cheeked babies
Kissed, fed, clothed
The gaps are filling
The lines becoming straight

Reflecting . . .
The goodbyes are endless
Nooks and crannies
Memories and plans
Every precious thing needs grief
Requires an ache
An honoring
A release

Settling . . .
Babes in bed
Tears come
Baptizing me again
Cleansing the dust of the day
Weary, stronger
God's love aimed at me
Winning every time

Resting . . .
Peace
Comfort
The Everlasting Arms wrapped 'round
Wandering thoughts are
Tucked into sleep
Hope comes to stand guard
Faith prepares a place
Soft, safe, warm
It is well with my soul

7

REFRAMING

MAKING SENSE OF YOUR STORY

Regardless of whether you reconcile with your husband or not, your life story is forever changed by the affair. Unpacking what happened, and what was real, is a necessary process for you to be able to move forward. The disorientation of the affair may make you feel like you will never have a handle on your life again, but I assure you that as long as you are walking with Jesus, stability and peace are in your future. The time and energy you spend reframing and rewriting your story will not be wasted. Whether you do that hard work with or without your husband, you have the task of redefining parts of your past, present, and future.

SEARCHING FOR ANSWERS

When a spouse is unfaithful, not only do you lose the certainty of a future with them, and connection with them in the present, but you also experience trauma that reaches backwards. Your past is as traumatized as your present and your future. The injury of the affair is not just the breaking of trust and covenant in one moment, the pain instantly reaches back to the genesis of your love. It strikes to the roots, sending shock waves of uncertainty to the very core of every memory you cherish. You're left with an avalanche of questions, cascading relentlessly through your mind. Every waking moment is full of tangled memories and all that was comfortable or special is now brought into question.

The Psalmist, King David, wrestled with his memories when he was betrayed by someone close to him:

> *If an enemy were insulting me, I could endure it; if a foe were rising against me, I could hide. But it is you, a man like myself, my companion, my close friend, with whom I once enjoyed sweet fellowship at the house of God, as we walked about among the worshipers.*
>
> Psalm 55:12-14 (NIV)

As he painfully expresses, being hurt from an enemy is one thing, but being deceived by a loved one is unbearable and causes a painful confusion about the past with that person.

No one can prepare for this kind of disorientation. Every single detail of daily life stirs up questions that echo on repeat in your mind. *Did he love me at our wedding? Was he lying when he told my father that he would always take care of me? Were there any pure moments of real connection? How long has he been lying to me?* The only person who can answer these questions is the one person you cannot trust right now with your shattered heart. You want to run to him with your hurt, but he is the source of it.

If your husband repents and you are able to restore with emotional safety, there may come a time when you will be able to sort through your past together and rewrite your story with one another. However, if you do end up healing on your own, there will be questions that you will face that are not easily answered.

In the initial stages of healing after the affair, I was so tempted to reach out to my husband for comfort, explanation, and truth. There were times I made myself vulnerable to him, only for that to be used as a weapon against me later. I had to force myself to not run back into the fire to soothe my burns. I had to find answers on my own.

As the questions piled up, I could not run from them. He was everywhere I looked—even when I closed my eyes, he haunted me. Normal, everyday things were turned into weapons, sharp and jagged. His favorite cereal in the cupboard, the inside jokes from our favorite show, the cologne I bought sitting on the counter, the pictures by my bedside of that trip to the coast, the note he wrote in my Bible. My home was a minefield. My memories felt unsafe. The tapestry of love and life and family was woven tight, and everything was unraveling. Nothing was untouched.

So many of my memories were *our* memories. Our life belonged to both of us. Yet now just the thought of him ripped me in two with pain. Instinct begged me to erase him, but how? To do that would be to erase myself. We were one. Our life was built together, intertwined and melded. Removing him would be like removing half of my skin. I had to find a way to keep what was precious to me and release what was too damaged.

PROCESSING YOUR MEMORIES

As you try to find solid ground on which to stand, your mind will scan through your past, trying to make sense of it. Imagine with me that your memories are printed pictures, each one representing an important moment embedded into your heart and mind. Some good, some bad, but they all belong together. Until now, most of your pictures during your marriage have been in one box. Let's call it the "We Love Each Other" box. Every time you used to look through this box, all your pictures were where they belonged, in the correct order, and you knew what to expect.

An affair dumps out the whole box, leaving pieces of your life and heart scattered all over the floor. The box is destroyed, crushed by the betrayal. It cannot be undone. You're devastated and overwhelmed, I know. The initial fear is that you've lost all of these precious moments, these building blocks of your reality. But the truth is that they are still there, on the floor. They just have changed.

Your memory pictures will never be sorted the same way they were. But hear me, sister: All of these pictures still belong to you. All of your memories are from your point of view. All of them are seen from your eyes—you are the photographer. You're asking, "Was it real?" I don't know what was real for him, and you can't know that for certain either. *But you do know what was real for you.*

Your job now is to pick up these memory pictures, one by one, and find them a new home. For me, I created a few new boxes in my mind. There was a "We Loved Each Other" and an "I Loved Him" box. Whenever I found a memory that I was confident was real and untouched by the affair, I put it in the "We Loved Each Other" box. When I wasn't sure if I could believe he was really there, really present, really honest, I put it in the "I Loved Him" box. That box got really full, really fast. There were and are so many memories where I just didn't know what he was feeling or thinking. At first that uncertainty caused such anxiety for me. But as I began to focus on what I did know, what I had experienced from my perspective, I began to redefine these moments. Many of them were diminished, or altered, but they were not lost.

You may have markers in your past where you feel confident and certain that your relationship was honest and real. For me, I believe that my wedding day was real. I believe the tears in his eyes when he saw me walking down the aisle were real. I believe he really, truly loved me in that moment. Regardless of what he told me during the divorce, I decided that this precious memory was real. It was empowering for me to decide that I had permission to define that day as pure and whole, with or without his agreement.

As I sorted, I also began to see the beauty of where I stood in all those memories. Rather than focusing on him, I started to concentrate on my own face. I looked at how I beamed at him when he got that diploma, crossed that finish line, shared his heart in that Bible study. I looked at the adoration in my eyes as I handed him our babies for the first time, as I watched him become a dad.

The love that flowed from my heart was real, real, real. I could still treasure those memories, but the point of view shifted focus.

TAKE YOUR TIME

It takes time to sift through all your memories. I found that it often wasn't an intentional task that I could sit down and work through. Memories aren't like that. A recollection can just hit you out of nowhere. Memories are triggered from all of our senses, and one smell or sound can bring them up, ready or not. In the early days, it is always visceral and painful. Your brain doesn't know where to put all these moments, and they can be triggers of the trauma.

You don't get to set the pace for the invasion of memories, which itself feels like a further violation. It's bad enough that you have to sort through this pain at all, but to not have control over when the pain hits? It is deeply unfair and unsettling. I remember being in the most inopportune places, like the grocery store, or picking up my kid from school, when a wave would hit. Sometimes I could function through it, other times I fell apart. I had to learn how to cope with each wave, and ultimately, I realized that 'keeping it together' was far less important than I thought it was. When your whole world is thrown upside down, you tend to care less about what strangers think of you.

Even though you don't get to choose when these memories will emerge, you do get to set the pace for the sorting. Some days I was hit with one memory after another, and it was grueling. I found that I didn't always have the virtue to sort them immediately, and at times, distractions were required. I had to learn to be gentle and patient with myself and to trust that I could sort the memory later if necessary—they had a way of coming back if they needed to find a place to land.

Some people are tempted to completely numb out and stall their rewriting process. Others feel guilty for taking a break at all. Be assured that you can strike a balance. Sometimes you will need to push through and really take some time to intentionally engage with your story. Other times, you'll need a break to refresh and refill your tank. There is no preset template for how long this process should take. Just be honest with yourself about where you are and where you want to go.

As you do the work of redefining your story, it will begin to settle into something you recognize and can cherish again. Some days will be a relentless work of unpacking, but your mind and heart will benefit from the work—every 'picture' you put away will help ease the sense of being scattered.

As I sorted and sorted, day after day, week after week, month after month, I began to be at peace with my memories. They stung less often. Every once in a while, I would get hit by a doozy, and my heart would catch in my throat, my body would flush with adrenaline. But those moments diminished as I began to accept this revised story of my life. When a memory that I had already dealt with resurfaced, it didn't hurt as much. The shock started to wear off, and I slowly began to recognize the new shape of my story.

I was able to see that God's promises to rebuild and remake my life were coming to fruition. The enemy had done his best to steal, kill, and destroy, but God was giving me life (John 10:10). God had allowed me to walk through suffering, and now He was lifting me up and restoring me to honor and strength (Psalm 71:20-21). The years that had been consumed by the enemy were being given back to me (Joel 2:24-26). God was sifting the rubble of my life and rebuilding something beautiful out of my broken places (Isaiah 61:4-7).

One day I was listening to the soundtrack of Wicked and heard the song "For Good" for the first time. I began weeping, as the truth of the lyrics hit me and resonated so deeply with the complicated feelings I was balancing every day. In response, I journaled about how I had been changed for the better because of the experience of knowing my husband:

It is so true—I have been changed for good. No going back, no restart. I am who I am because of the love and the loneliness, the nurture and the neglect, the fun and the faithlessness. And ultimately, I am so grateful to him. I wouldn't change where I have been or where I am now. It may seem foolish, but reality is all I have and I want to treasure it. It feels strange and lonely, but so alive. This is my story, and I don't want to shy away from living it.

It takes a lot of courage to walk away from brokenness with your head held high. It takes even more courage to walk away with memories of the wholeness still intact, remembering and honoring what was lost. It would be easier to say the whole marriage was a sham. That he fooled me the entire time. That it was destined to fail—a mistake, a statistic, a doomed start. That he was bad, I was good. But that's a LIE. We were in love, we both carefully decided to make a holy covenant, we created a family. Most of our history is chock full of blessing and goodness. He was my best friend and he did a lot of things right. It's hard to reconcile that truth with the sheer nightmare of the last few years. But I HAVE to reconcile it as I heal. It was my life, and it was beautiful. I loved that man, and part of my forgiveness is recognizing how much he changed me. For better or for worse, I get to decide.

I was all in. The fact that I'm all out now doesn't change that.

It is over, but it left a mark. I get to choose every day whether that mark becomes beauty or bitterness.

It was not easy to hold the tension between the light and the dark in my memory. It will no doubt take great strength and perspective to hold this wide array of feelings and truths for you, as well. But as you expand your hurting heart to hold the good and the bad, allow yourself to retain what was whole, without denying what was so deeply broken. The truth of your story includes it all, and it would be a tragedy to lose any part of it. You cannot afford to live a lie. You deserve to live in the full and honest truth, with all its imperfections.

PRAYER

God, thank You for being with me as I rewrite my story. This is never what I wanted for myself. There is so much confusion, disappointment, and unanswered questions. Thank You for walking with me as I sort through each memory. You were with me then, and You saw it all. Comfort me and strengthen me as I walk in this present moment, and as I explore my past.

APPLICATION

1. Find three memories that you cherished before the affair. Take your time. Hold them in your mind, one by one. Breathe. Let it hurt. Then, look at your face in the memory, and tell me about what you see in yourself.

2. As you do the hard work of redefining your past, what contradictions are hard to hold together?

3. What is one way you have been brave in this season? How can you honor yourself for that?

Perched on the razor edge
Suspended but for a time
The winds of change blow strong
A choice must be made

Right? Left? Which risk to take?
For there is no such thing
As a safe descent

The lie of the victim whispers
"Let chance decide"
But courage is in the choosing
And the peaceful smile before the fall

The Lord of ledges made me
God of gravity designed it all
The Spirit of my story is here
Never to leave or forsake

What is fear, then?
A baseless accusation
A foolish haze
A fictitious terror

Jump, baby girl
Feel the weightless glory of living
The acceleration of decision
And the holy joy of being held throughout

8

DECISIONS

MOVING FORWARD WITH WISDOM

Navigating this season of your life will require making a staggering number of decisions you never thought you would have to make. I remember being flooded with so many thoughts and questions that varied from minor to life altering—it was overwhelming. *Do I need to pull out money into a separate account? What do I tell my kids, and when? Should I get a different job? What should I say to my pastor? How long do I wait to see if he gets an STI test before I should get one myself? Should I hire a lawyer?*

Regardless of where you are on your journey, it's likely that you carry the weight of all these questions, the answers to which will impact and define your future. While I cannot tell you the *right* decisions to make, my hope is to give you some tools and guiding questions that will help you move forward with greater peace and confidence. Your story is unique, and your choices are ultimately between you and the Lord. He is the One you will need to prioritize seeking and spending time with as you process the decisions before you.

WAIT ON THE LORD

One piece of advice that my mom has given me throughout the years stood out during this time: if you don't know what to do, wait. It became my strategy. If I didn't have an answer, if I didn't have clarity, I would wait until I knew.

Now, let's be honest. Sometimes 'knowing' feels a lot more like guessing. My certainty meter had been damaged by the mind-bending betrayal I was walking through, but somewhere deep down, I still knew that the person most qualified to make the decisions about my life and my kids was myself. No one else could know what to do with my life more than I did. I knew how to hear God's voice, and when the time came to make a decision, if there was a feeling of resolve or peace, even if it was small, that let me know it was time to move forward and choose. If I didn't have that resolve or peace, I needed to pray and wait until it came.

Waiting is hard. Especially when we know that making a decision might give us some relief from the torment, we can be tempted to rush. And there may be some decisions that really do need to be made immediately, to secure safety for you, or perhaps children involved. But most of the time, waiting benefits you, giving you time to get the information and perspective you need to make wise choices.

I was not used to making big decisions by myself. My husband and I were a team, and I was much more confident making decisions together. But with my faith in him broken, I had to learn to trust myself. You might also find yourself unsure of your capability, and this new responsibility may have you feeling unprepared, uncertain, and overwhelmed. This is where prayer and waiting on the Lord come in.

In the book of James, we are instructed to ask God for wisdom when we need it:

> *If you need wisdom, ask our generous God, and he will give it to you. He will not rebuke you for asking. But when you ask him, be sure that your faith is in God alone. Do not waver, for a person with divided loyalty is as unsettled as a wave of the sea that is blown and tossed by the wind.*
>
> *James 1:5-6*

God knows your need for wisdom. He is gracious and generous towards you, and He wants to give you what you need to make the right decisions for your situation—He has answers for you! But this verse also illustrates what happens when we doubt that God will speak, or distrust what He says. As you process the choices before you, make sure your loyalty is set on Him. Your confidence in Him is what will keep you settled and steady. You are already in the middle of a storm, and the waves and wind are doing their best to toss you around. When you feel shaken and unsteady, return to God once again and ask Him for wisdom. Believe that He has it for you, and wants to comfort and still your heart.

As you walk out one impossible decision after another, know also that grace is covering your steps. Your decisions matter, but there is mercy to cover your mistakes—you will have the opportunity to make new choices tomorrow if you get it wrong today. There is truly no perfect rule book for your situation. God wants to lead you step-by-step, but you will not get everything right. That is okay. You were not prepared for this to be your life, and you are not expected to know exactly what to do in each moment. Ask the Lord, press into His presence, and trust that He will guide you in His timing.

As you wait on the Lord, you will also find that there is more to your relationship with Him than just access to wisdom about the choices in front of you. The same God who beautifully reveals Himself throughout the Bible, from one generation to the next, is the God who is writing your story with you. Being close and connected to Him is the ultimate blessing, in and of itself.

These are some of the biggest decisions you will make in your life, and there is no one-size-fits-all solution. You may be weighing whether to attempt to restore the marriage or to pursue a divorce. Or maybe you are in the middle of a divorce and determining custody of children, or how to divide financial assets. Every situation is unique, and while we can see clear black and white directives in God's Word about many things, a lot of these decisions exist in a gray area that requires God's grace and guidance to discern. What was true for my circumstances may not be true for yours, and you can trust that God will individually lead you through all these choices. As you process the options in front of you, I believe there are several key principles that apply to every situation.

GET WISE COUNSEL

No one fully understands the specifics of your situation like you do. Even people like myself, who have walked through a similar fire, can never see every detail, or understand the complexity and nuance of your story and relationship. You are the expert on your heart and life. However, while there is no one person who can make these decisions for you, God designed us to operate best in community. You have blind spots. There are things you cannot see clearly from your vantage point. Even the fact that you are in such deep pain means that you need to balance out your decisions with other people you trust.

The Bible has a lot to say about getting advice and perspective from godly people. In Proverbs, we see several key passages that emphasize the benefits of getting counsel. Proverbs 11 teaches us that where there is no guidance we will fall, but "in an abundance of counselors there is safety" (v.14, ESV). Similarly, Proverbs 19 exhorts us to be willing to listen to advice and accept instruction, so that we can gain wisdom (v.20), while Proverbs 24 ascribes strength and might to those who possess wisdom and knowledge, telling us wise guidance enables us to wage our war, "and in abundance of counselors there is victory" (vv.5-6, ESV).

All these things—safety, wisdom, strength, might, waging your war, victory—are exactly what you need as you make decisions about your future. Who doesn't want to wrap up their decisions with those promises? Just reading these proverbs can infuse you with hope that you are not alone, and strengthen your confidence in your future.

Since these are all results from seeking and heeding wise counsel, it makes sense that the opposite is true about going it alone. When you make decisions without bringing godly people in to weigh in, you get the opposite result. You can fall into danger, foolishness, weakness, exhaustion, giving up on your war, and defeat. That is not what God wants for you! He wants you to follow His lead and listen well to the counsel of wise people around you, so that you can walk into safety, strength and victory. It may take a while, there may be losses along the way, but that is God's heart for your life. He is making a way before you, and it includes the wisdom of other people in your life.

Note that in these verses, God does not instruct us to confer with just one person, but a wide and balanced group. Counselors are plural. You need to hear more than one perspective. There will be nuggets of truth and wisdom that you gather from several people during this season, and the sum of their counsel is better than just one single source.

I also want to give another warning at this point: Be careful who you let speak into your life. You do need counselors, but specifically *wise* counselors. Not everyone is equally qualified and it will be important that you measure every piece of advice you are given by the Word of God. I will be straight with you, sometimes people, even in the church, are just so uncomfortable with the level of darkness involved in an affair that they cannot see it for what it is. I have worked with women whose husbands have been convicted of raping other women, child pornography, and other unspeakable sins, and they have still had other people minimize, overlook, or not believe them. This means you may get bad advice at times. People are not perfect, and they make mistakes. It is common for others to encounter the shock of a scandal and respond with denial, and most move through their own processing of it at a slower pace than you will, since only you are at the center of it. Some people may not be able to keep up with the reality of your situation at a pace that is helpful. Even with the best of intentions, people can miss the mark. Having a diverse and balanced group of people you are getting counsel from will help protect against misplaced advice.

The goal in getting good, godly counsel is to find balance. As I have walked with women through these tough decisions, I often encourage them to think about an old school scale, with two sides. Some counsel may fall on one side of a decision, and some on the other side. Your own thoughts and feelings will be mixed as well. It can be discouraging to hear conflicting opinions, and to feel divided in your own heart, but as you add perspectives to the scale, it will become more apparent where wisdom leads. It is important to consider how much weight to assign to different people, based on your trust in them, the authority they hold in your life, and their connection to the Lord. For instance, if you have trusted and wise pastors, they should hold more weight than your friend who loves you but is a hot mess. Some people should carry more weight, and eventually you will sense that wisdom is leaning towards one side of a decision.

In addition to counsel from family, friends, and church leaders, it was immensely helpful for me to have professional counseling as I recovered. A trained counselor does not focus much on giving advice but rather directs you to the right questions to ask of yourself, and the answers that you may already know but have difficulty seeing. My therapists throughout the years have helped me navigate the landscape of my trauma with helpful tools that most people did not have.

I also recommend that every woman walking through this trauma assembles a recovery team, full of people you trust and admire, who are committed to your healing and obedience to the Lord. Beware of selecting people that will just tell you what you want to hear, or who encourage you to respond in worldly ways, rather than godly ones. There were several friends that I initially confided in, but had to pull back from after a while. For instance, as I was working on forgiving my husband, one person's bitterness toward him constantly steered the conversation. I loved her and was grateful for her fierce protectiveness over me, but I knew that I needed to process with someone who would support my hard work of forgiveness, rather than someone who was making it more difficult. Some relationships within your recovery team may ebb and flow, and that is okay. You will not please everyone, and that is not your job. Your job is to follow the Lord, and trust that His way is best.

The most powerful partners in my recovery were those people who listened well, gave their honest perspective when asked, and were committed to supporting me regardless of which decision I came to. They were more interested in me being at peace with the outcome than their opinion being right or having me follow their advice, and their trust in my ability to hear and follow God gave me courage and dignity. I encourage you to give more weight to those kinds of counselors, who show humility and grace during your difficult decisions.

As you assemble your recovery team, ask yourself the following:

Who do I trust to be careful with my heart in this season?

Who do I trust to tell me my blind spots, even if I don't like hearing it?

Is there someone God is leading me to talk to who I am avoiding because I am afraid of what they might say?

Is my team balanced with people who will comfort *and* challenge me?

Is there anyone I am seeking counsel from who has not proven to be wise, or is hindering my healing or forgiveness? How can I gracefully distance myself from their counsel?

Ultimately, the choices fall to you. No one else has the right or the responsibility to decide on your behalf. But as you gather wisdom from your community, you will be more confident and supported in your decisions.

CHOOSE TO ACT, NOT REACT

Motivation and intention matter in decision making. You can make the same decision with two different motives, and experience very different outcomes. We cannot truly know others' intentions, but we can be honest about our own. It is important to recognize that God sees into our hearts and holds us accountable for our inner motivations.

For instance, filing for divorce in a rage as an attempt to hurt your husband is completely different from prayerfully deciding to file the paperwork (or respond to his paperwork) with peace and forgiveness in your heart. Likewise, deciding to stay with your husband because you are afraid of being alone, or because you believe that you are broken and unlovable, is a completely different experience than prayerfully deciding to stay with dignity, courage, and strong boundaries in your heart. Neither outcome is automatically right or wrong, but either one can be made for the wrong reasons. You should not stay or go based on fear, anger, or insecurity. It is totally normal to feel all those things, but instead of reacting to them, pause before making decisions when you are flooded with feeling. Give these emotions space to exist and make room for them to pass through. When you are feeling steadier and more confident, reassess your intentions and move forward with motivations you are proud of.

When you have been traumatized, it is totally understandable that your initial response is to react, protect yourself, and get away from the pain and danger. But when you are making life-shaping decisions, you want to take steps to make sure your direction is determined by your values, not by your reaction to someone else. Reacting gives power away to others, but when you respond based on who you are and what God is leading you to, the power stays with you and God.

I understand that it is very difficult to deal with a person so close to you who is apparently willing to care so little for your heart, your health, and your life. Many women that I coach find themselves desperate to make choices that will steer the adulterer toward truth, safety, cooperation, etc. But I remind them that they are not responsible to alter his choices, they are only responsible for their own. Try not to make a decision based on how you think he will react—your motives should be rooted in following the Lord, not in manipulating your husband into doing the right thing. If you make a decision, or have a conversation, in which you represent yourself and the Lord well, I consider that a win, regardless of what your husband does in response.

Here are some questions to help you measure the wisdom of your motivation as you make decisions:

Am I making this choice to get a response from someone else?

Does my attitude in making this decision reflect who I want to be in Christ?

Am I valuing myself correctly in this decision? Am I valuing others correctly?

Am I making this decision out of fear, anger, or insecurity? If so, how can I process those feeling *before* making this decision?

One of the most empowering shifts that occurs in women walking this road, is when they discover their own agency and autonomy. My prayer is that you make choices that flow from who you are in Christ, rather than from a desire to change or manage someone else. Keeping your conscience clear before the Lord is the most freeing and liberating path you can choose, knowing that no matter what anyone else does, you can stand before Him with your head held high.

CHOOSE YOUR HARD, FIND YOUR HEALING

At some point you will likely face the decision whether or not to file for a divorce. Sister, if that choice was made for you, and you felt like you didn't have a say in the matter—divorce was forced upon you—I'm sorry that you experienced further disempowerment. But I want you to know these same truths apply to your situation; you can still find healing. However, if the weight of this decision rests on your shoulders alone, you need to know that the Word of God says that once your covenant has been broken, the choice is yours—you are free to go or to stay. If you stay, let it be because God is calling and gracing you to. There is no place like the will of God. But do not stay out of fear of man, or out of a false guilt. There are biblical grounds for you to divorce or to restore, so the question is not whether or not you will be in sin. The question is, *Which way is God leading you?*

There is a popular quote going around social media, whose author is unknown: "Marriage is hard. Divorce is hard. Choose your hard." While it may be an over-simplification, there is an element of truth that is undeniable. Both choices include a long list of things that are hard.

Divorce is excruciating. There is permanent damage on children involved. It is expensive and stressful. It can be drawn out and will always leave a mark on your life. There is a chance that you could be hurt in a future relationship, or be alone for longer than you desire.

Divorce can also mean freedom from extended abuse and protection from the risk of the same person hurting you again. If you walk it out with God, it can be a testimony of His faithfulness and strength. You can be divorced and fully healed.

Restoration is excruciating. You are never guaranteed success, and the risk is huge. It is emotionally costly and stressful. It can also be drawn out and will always leave a mark on your life. There is a chance you can restore and then walk through unfaithfulness again later.

Restoration can also mean a deeper connection than you have

ever had with your spouse and protection for your kids from the chaos of two homes. Again, if you walk it out with God, it can be a testimony of His faithfulness and strength. You can restore a marriage and be fully healed.

Both paths are painful. Both paths are difficult. Both paths hold risk. I wish there was a clear, pain-free exit strategy from this, but there honestly is not. I would be lying to you if I said one road is safer than the other. They both hold dangers and costs that you should not have to face. There is no easy way out of this, but God is with you. Being fully committed and submitted to His voice in this process is vital. He knows which path will lead you home. There is safety and security in *Him*, no matter which route you take to healing.

I have often likened a woman faced with the decision to reconcile or divorce after an affair to a mother who is faced with the decision to leave her injured child on life support or not, after a brutal attack on her child's life. Regardless of what she chooses, her community should offer unconditional support, love, care, and trust in her. If the child does not survive, no one should level the responsibility on her shoulders.

Too often, well-intentioned people put themselves in the role of the doctor when they are not actually qualified to measure the situation. Perhaps they can see that there's a heartbeat and they decide that the child is alive and well, when in reality, the doctor has sadly announced that the child is brain dead with no chance of life outside of artificial support. Or conversely, maybe the child looks lifeless to the common eye, but the doctor is encouraging the mother with hopeful news about what is happening inside and urging her to give it more time. In these cases, God is the doctor and the only One worthy of instructing the bereaved woman. The rest of us should be in the waiting room—crying, praying, bringing coffee, caring for other children, donating funds, and hugging the hurting woman.

Sister, I trust you to hear the voice of your Great Physician. God knows your situation inside and out. You are being faced with impossible choices, but only you and God can truly know which path to take. Be assured, both paths can, and will, lead to healing if you are walking with Jesus. There is hope with Him, no matter which one He directs you to take. As you surrender your pain and your process to Him, He will continue to heal and restore every layer of your life. It takes the pressure off, to realize that you cannot go wrong with Him. Wait on Him, listen to His people in your life, root yourself in His Word, and trust that He is with you and for you as He guides you down this difficult road.

PRAYER

God, I recognize my need of You. You have the wisdom I need for every decision in front of me. Teach me to wait on You and hear Your voice. Help me to follow peace, and not fear, as I walk with You on this difficult road. I thank You that Your grace will continue to cover me, and that when I make mistakes Your mercy is still new every morning.

APPLICATION

1. Think of a decision that you are facing right now. What does waiting on the Lord as you process it look like?

2. What is one decision or conversation that you have had with your husband since the affair where you were led by who you are in Christ, not by their reaction? How did that feel?

3. If you're considering divorce or reconciliation, ask yourself: What would I be risking by choosing divorce? What would I be risking by choosing to repair the marriage? How can I invite God in to protect me in the midst of these risks?

It's not about
Revenge

There is no
Getting even

Just a choice -
Life or Death

I'll take this pain,
And raise you
One belly laugh!

You can laugh too,
If you want

Life is funny

Laughter is abundant
There is enough for all

We can make it,
Manufacture our own
In our gut

No one can force you
Towards laughter
Or keep you from it

Yeah, I am crying
This really hurts

BUT

Nothing can
Take
My joy

No, thanks

My joy
Is
Untouchable

Do what you will
Think your thoughts
Have your way

Take things
Take space
Take money

Those are not
Mine,
Stewardess that
I am

Love
        Joy
Peace

Patience

Kindness

Goodness

Faithfulness

Gentleness

Self Control

These are my fruit
From His Spirit inside of me,
Life blood of my soul

I already ate
This God-food
Nourishes deep

Please
Share a meal
There's plenty
For you too

9

DIVORCE

SAYING A GRACIOUS GOODBYE

If your marriage has died and you are either planning to, or have already, filed the divorce death certificate, I want to share with you some of the lessons I learned as I accepted the reality that there was no resurrection miracle ahead for my marriage. If your marriage is in the process of being revived, and you need to protect its recovery by not 'going there', please feel free to skip this chapter. But whether the hard choice God has led you to is reconciliation or divorce, I pray you find wisdom here that will help you guard your own heart and the hearts of those you love as you navigate the aftermath of adultery.

BEING MISUNDERSTOOD

The decision to divorce is not something that someone in your position takes lightly. It is very likely, unfortunately, that you have people in your life who will not understand what this decision has cost you. Sadly, many Christian family members, friends, leaders and counselors are ill-equipped to offer the support you may need during this time. I was fortunate enough to have the vast majority of my family, friends, and church offer me full support, but many of the women I have coached do not have that story. And even though I received judgement from very few people, when I did, it still hurt deeply and was another layer of pain I had to work through.

I want to encourage you that the decision to divorce your husband as an acknowledgment of a broken covenant is not lack of faith, or an act of disobedience. If anyone says otherwise, you can remind them of what we believe: Burial does not limit God. Lazarus walked out of the tomb, while the rest of the bodies buried there did not walk out with him. God chooses when and how to answer our prayers with the miracle. You do not have to live with a dead body to walk in faith and obedience.

If you are being unsupported, or facing unfair judgement about the divorce, my heart is with you. That is a secondary wound on top of the deep relational trauma you have endured, and it is not fair. I encourage you to seek out safe, trusted people for you to heal with, even if they are not who you have typically reached out to before. Some relationships may need more space or may need to end altogether for you to find peace and healing in your future. I believe it is important to not make rash decisions in your pain, but as you prayerfully seek God's wisdom on how to rebuild your life, He will guide you on who to keep close, who to keep at a distance, and who to let go.

As I have healed, I realize that most people who are unsupportive of a necessary and biblical divorce are often well intentioned, but misinformed and uncomfortable with the reality that some relationships can be broken beyond repair. Nothing is impossible with God, but the truth is that many, many people choose to not invite God into their lives and choices. The 'with God' piece is essential. If your ex-husband broke covenant and is not walking with God, you are not called to walk with him. Your escape was a mercy from God. Some people refuse to accept that, but rather than argue with those individuals, I found it helpful to first find healing and stability. Later I was able to engage in such conversations with confidence, grace, and dignity. Remember: you do not owe every single person an explanation. If your heart is clean and clear before the Lord, find rest in the knowledge that someone else's misunderstanding does not define you, and comfort in the truth that He *never* misunderstands us. As David declared:

> *You have searched me, Lord, and you know me. You know when I sit and when I rise; you perceive my thoughts from afar. You discern my going out and my lying down; you are familiar with all my ways. Before a word is on my tongue you, Lord, know it completely. You hem me in behind and before, and you lay your hand upon me. Such knowledge is too wonderful for me, too lofty for me to attain.*
>
> *Psalm 139:1-6 (NIV)*

He sees you, sister, and He knows and understands you completely. God also knows the truth and while others may not believe you, if you have His covering, there is nothing else you need.

I must admit that I often struggle with leaning too much on other people to tell me I'm on track, or that my heart is pure, or that I'm being obedient to God. The minute I am misunderstood, I get to see just how hard I'm leaning towards people rather than God. Do I find my balance quickly? Or do I fall face first, having been propped up by a false sense of security? It hurts, but it's an opportunity to lean back into Jesus. Jesus modeled the complete dependence we need to have on the Father, through the Spirit. He was misunderstood at every turn, but it did not turn Him. He did not defend Himself in pride but submitted Himself in full humility to God (1 Peter 2:23).

Jesus' submission did not mean it was not painful for Him to be misunderstood. With tears in His eyes, He cried out over Jerusalem (Luke 19:41-44). He longed for her to really see Him, and He did everything possible to reveal Himself in truth and love. But He still let her choose. He let her be wrong. You have let your ex-husband be wrong, accepted his choices, and you have said a painful goodbye. Now, you may need to let other people be wrong too, and just as the Lord graced you with the strength to forgive and release your ex-husband, He will enable you to forgive and release them also.

CHANGING THE PASSWORDS

Grief is always messy, but the grief of divorce has complex layers to it. You mourn the loss of someone you love, but you also have been released from being committed and connected to someone who is actively harming you, and there is often a sense of deep relief in that. Yet you also miss them or find yourself longing for them. That is normal, too. Even though they were, and perhaps still are, the source of so much pain and damage in your life, they were someone you loved deeply. Regardless of the mix of emotions, one thing is certain: The relationship is forever changed. And because of this, some of your patterns and behaviors also need to alter.

One of the first things I did during the separation was to change the password to my personal information. Because I had uncovered financial risk to myself, I got my own bank account, instinctively protecting myself from further exposure and exploitation. As I proceeded with the divorce, I realized that changing the passwords was a symbol that applied to more areas of my life than just money. If this man was no longer my husband, I also needed to change the passwords to my heart.

This was not an easy thing to do, and it was not something I figured out overnight. But access to my inner thoughts and feelings was a privilege of marriage, and once that access was violated, it was up to me to restrict it. At first it felt wrong. My heart had been open to him for years and years. It was something that we shared and blocking him from it made me feel uncomfortable, dishonest, and even guilty. Out of habit, I would share what I was thinking with him. He knew what to say and do to get a reaction from me, and I kept giving him password hints.

Over time, I realized that I needed to redefine the relationship. Because we had children together, I knew that I would need to communicate with him regularly for years to come, but it could not be the same as it had been. I needed to find a different way to relate to this person who felt like a stranger in the ghost-shell of a man I used to know.

To keep with the banking analogy, we had to set up different 'accounts'. We would need to transfer some things (information, our children) back and forth occasionally, but that did not mean that I had to give him the password to come and go as he pleased. I did not owe him the freedom and the right to withdraw at any time. Divorcing him took his name off the account of my life, but if I was giving him the password, I had some responsibility when he withdrew more than I wanted. It was up to me to protect myself from him emotionally and put up the boundaries I needed to heal. For me, that meant not telling him how I was feeling about *anything*. I limited our communication to text and email and made it clear that I would discuss the children and other important details regarding the divorce, but nothing else. There were a few times when I broke my own rules, but it always stung me in the end. When this happened, it was time to change the password again.

It is a huge adjustment to change the way you interact with someone who has been your most intimate partner and friend. Give yourself grace and time. Just remind yourself that if he is not your husband, *he is not your husband*. Do not treat him like he is.

It was helpful for me, especially in the early days, to imagine that I was someone else's wife. I had not yet met my future husband, nor was I open to dating until I was officially divorced and had found deeper healing, but the idea that I was being faithful to *someone else* by putting up those internal and external boundaries was helpful for me. I would ask myself, *How would I respond to him right now if I were married to another man?* I wouldn't confide in him my fears, I would not let him hug me, I would not let him tell me he misses me. It would be inappropriate if I were married to someone else *because it was already inappropriate*. When the marriage is over, all marital connection and obligation are dissolved. It takes some time to evaluate what parts of the relationship are now off-limits, but it is worth the work of setting those boundaries.

Maybe you're not ready to even think of another man. I totally get that. If you've been married for a substantial amount of time, it may be difficult to identify as single again. Many of the women I coach find it helpful to consider themselves as married to Jesus Himself. Whatever is helpful mentally for you to do to disconnect from your ex-husband, give yourself grace to try it.

God Himself made major adjustments to His relationship with Israel when He chose to divorce her for her adultery. He changed their communication style, refusing to listen to her cries for help anymore (Jeremiah 11:10-11, 14-15). He also banished her from the sacred space where they used to connect in His temple, saying "What right has my beloved in my house, when she has done many vile deeds?" (Jeremiah 11:15, ESV). The marital rights and access were revoked when the covenant was broken, and there should be no shame or hesitation for you to enact new and firm boundaries. This is a necessary rearranging of your life.

Your ex-husband no longer has the right of access to your heart or your life. You are released from your responsibility to him as a wife. However, he is also released from responsibility to you as a husband. Some women struggle to lower their expectations, even after a divorce, and suffer disappointment when their ex-husband does not meet their needs. I understand that it may take some time and practice to adjust to your new roles, but I urge you to not expect much from your ex-husband, to save yourself from unnecessary disappointment. To quote the old Al-Anon analogy, "Don't go to the hardware store looking for a loaf of bread." This man did not measure up to the standard of a husband and is no longer in that role. Divorcing him gave you the protection and distance you need, but it also removed him from a place of responsibility to treat you as a husband should.

FINALIZED

The finalization of the divorce is an important milestone in the healing journey. Typically, the legal proceedings tend to lag behind where you are in your heart. For me, once I made the decision to stop waiting and to file the death certificate of my dead marriage, internally I was divorced. The following months of paperwork and waiting were an interesting and awkward limbo. Being 'done' was a big step and I journaled about how it felt for the divorce to be final.

> *It came in the most understated way. A phone call. In a parking lot. "Ruth, I wanted to call and let you know that you are divorced."*
>
> *I threw my head back and let out a big, mirth-filled, "WOO-HOO!" The relief! The closure! The validation of what has been true for months inside of me: It is over.*
>
> *When I tell people, I can see that they are conflicted. Should they congratulate? Offer condolences? It is not a natural or happy thing, per se. Divorce: A complete separation between two things. Two things that were once one. It truly is terrible. It reeks of sin, of lies, of destruction. It is opposite of Shalom, of God's Way, of our human ache for Divine Union.*
>
> *But I was created for love. I was designed to be united to a human who is able and willing to unite with me. That has not been reality for quite some time. Divorce, ugly though it is, set me free and brought my life back into the light. My outsides can once again reflect my insides. I am no longer bound to humiliation, confusion, and abuse. There is clear separation, and that creates the safety I need to continue loving him well. Loving differently, surely, but it is love.*
>
> *It may seem surprising that the finality has not been heavy emotionally for me. I am not sad, discouraged, or regretful. I am excited, hopeful, and grateful! I have been working my tail off to grieve this thing. I front loaded this journey with intense and honest processing. And now I get to dance and rejoice in my freedom!*
>
> *It seems fitting that I should move out of my little home this month. It has*

DIVORCE

been a year. A year since things started to completely unravel. Since things fell apart and finally fell into place at the same time. So much has happened in this house. My heart was broken here. I uncovered the truth here. I wept and reeled and vomited here. I lost twenty pounds, like a reverse pregnancy, overcome with mo[u]rning sickness that led to the birth of my new Self. This is the place where my tribe tended my wounds. This is the place I established new rhythms, new normal with my children. This is the place I learned acceptance. It was in these mirrors that I saw myself. Crying, searching, resolving, rebuilding. This is where I wrote my heart out in song and prose. This is where my most raw music was born. God was known here as I braved my storms, as I fell apart, as I gained speed. He has covered and blessed and transformed.

Lord, may I never forget what I learned here, in this place and time. The density and intensity of this year is breathtaking. This next season will likely be a much different pace and texture. But I am so grateful for the new strength and truth I carry with me. Any doubts I had about God's character, power, or goodness are dissolved.

> *"I'm convinced: You can do anything and everything. Nothing and no one can upset your plans. You asked, 'Who is this muddying the water, ignorantly confusing the issue, second-guessing my purposes?' I admit it. I was the one. I babbled on about things far beyond me, made small talk about wonders way over my head. You told me, 'Listen, and let me do the talking. Let me ask the questions. You give the answers.'*
>
> *I admit I once lived by rumors of you; now I have it all firsthand—from my own eyes and ears! I'm sorry—forgive me. I'll never do that again, I promise! I'll never again live on crusts of hearsay, crumbs of rumor."* Job 42:1-6 (MSG)

Nothing but my pain and brokenness could have brought me so completely to my knees. So even as I am divorced from my past, my first love, my original dream, I am married to Beauty, Truth, and Hope. I am scarred and walk with a little limp, but my Love calls me His beautiful bride.

Your experience with the finalization of your divorce may not be the same as mine. Regardless of whether you feel relief or pain, sadness or joy, freedom or burden, my prayer for you is that you will find some closure when the divorce is finalized. I also pray that you will be able to look back on your journey and see how far you have come, and how near the Lord has been to your broken heart.

BEST EX EVER

I never, ever imagined myself as a divorced person. I think that is fairly true of most divorced people. It was unwanted and unexpected, but there I was, faced with the reality that my marriage was over and I was on my own.

Because of the work I had done, and continue to do, with forgiveness and healing, my goal was clear as a divorced woman: I wanted to be the best ex ever.

It is counter-cultural, to be sure. We live in a world that encourages you to fight for what is yours, make them pay, get them back for what they've put you through. Believe me, I had to fight those urges too. Some days, all these years later, I still do! But as God touched my life, guarded my heart, and brought me the deepest healing and transformation I could have ever hoped for, I knew that I owed it to God to do this His way.

So, what does being the 'best ex ever' look like?

It does *not* look like giving your ex-husband everything he wants. There will be countless decisions where you will not agree. Even the word 'divorce' makes it clear that you are taking different paths. Derived from the Latin word *divertere*, where we get our word 'divert', we get the meaning of turning in different directions. There is no way to be in complete unity with a man who is not your husband. You are not obligated to keep submitting to one another, as is necessary in marriage. You are called to be submitted to God alone. Obviously, this man is headed in a direction that you do not want to go, so do not be surprised when you disagree.

So, if it is not about agreement, what is being the best ex ever about? It is about *how* you disagree. It means submitting to God, and allowing Him to direct every conversation, decision, and attitude. Not out of trying to please your ex-husband, or out of fear of legal retaliation, or any such thing. Your motivation must be wanting to please God, it must come out of your fear of the Lord—your reverence for Him. Only He can give you the perspective and insight to navigate your disagreements without entering into sin and bitterness.

Becoming the best ex I could be took some learning and adjusting. Being a godly wife was something I understood. I had a template and a reference in Scripture and in my life with the marriages I admired. However, being a godly ex-wife was something I had never considered becoming. But when I was honest with myself, I knew the Spirit was showing me what I needed to do in my context. So, when it came to splitting up the finances, or what to do with the children, or how to communicate, I had a sense of what was fair and reasonable. Is it what my ex wanted? No. Is it what my flesh wanted? No. It was usually somewhere in the middle, right where Jesus was calling me.

To this day, my goal has not changed. Over the eight years since the divorce, there have been many disagreements and conflicts that have challenged my resolve. Through the waves of adrenaline, triggers, fear and frustration, my job is the same: God has called me to honor *Him* in how I respond to every detail. I cannot control my ex-husband, but I can control my responses.

We have been released from loving our exes as a husband, but we are not released from loving them altogether. There are several different words for 'love' in the Bible, and while the romantic erotic love, *eros*, is no longer appropriate in this relationship, the unconditional, unearned *agape* love of God is what we are called to give. Jesus commands us to love our enemies (Matthew 5:43-48).

Whether you consider your ex your enemy or not, God is expecting you to love him in a new way, no matter how hard it may be.

The Lord has called you and I to a high road. A very, very high road. I am reminded of a drive I took in college, high up in the rugged Rocky Mountains of Colorado, to Pike's Peak. As the road climbed, the air thinned and I became dizzy and out of breath. The high altitude is notorious for causing nose bleeds and for exhausting even elite athletes. Sometimes it feels like that, sister. The high road can cost you. It is not the easy road. But I promise you, the view is worth it, and you will not regret being closer to the Lord up here.

THE CHILDREN

If you have children with your ex-husband, I want to encourage you that the same God who is walking with you, offering you healing and hope, is with them and for them. This road will not be easy for them either, but they are covered by the grace and mercy of God, and He is working on their behalf. There are also things that *you* can do to shield them and aid their healing, and as their mother, it is both your privilege and responsibility to do so.

One of the most painful parts of my divorce was knowing that the death of this marriage would hurt my children for years to come. Something precious had been taken from them that I could not restore. Watching their confusion and hurt was breathtakingly painful for me. I was desperate to do *anything* in my power to alleviate their pain.

I had to remember and leverage that desire to protect them in the moments where my white-hot rage broiled against their father. I had to protect them from *myself* and my attitudes. As tempted as I was to let the anger spill out, I knew it would burn them. I had to guard my mouth relentlessly. I want to be very honest and firm on this: There is absolutely no excuse for any parent to place the burden of a divorce on a child. And I mean *any* parent, even the victim. Now, I understand, deeply, that your pain and trauma from your ex-husband is real. You deserve support and a safe place to process. But it is not with your children.

Every piece of research I have read, and all the personal stories I have heard from adult children of divorce, confirms that it is *always* damaging to a child to hear one parent talk down about the other. Even if the criticism is deserved. Even if the facts are correct. It hurts the child more than it hurts the ex, so I encourage you to create a zero-tolerance rule for yourself of bad-mouthing your child's other parent. No matter what.

The temptation is real, and it is not new. Christians from the beginning of the faith have struggled with controlling their tongues. As Jesus' brother James said, "Sometimes [the tongue] praises our Lord and Father, and sometimes it curses those who have been made in the image of God. And so blessing and cursing come pouring out of the same mouth. Surely, my brothers and sisters, this is not right!" (James 3:9-10). You cannot bless your child and curse the one you created them with. You must bless them both, or curse them both.

Certainly, there are times when a child needs to understand appropriate boundaries on how to keep themselves safe. I have walked with women who have valid concerns regarding physical and sexual abuse of their children, and those children need to be equipped with the knowledge and tools to advocate for themselves, and a safe line of communication about what is happening with the other parent. A professional counselor and abuse advocate is essential in these circumstances, to know what information is helpful to the child, and what produces more harm than good. It is not an easy thing to dissect, and you may make mistakes. But even in these extreme circumstances, the children deserve every effort on your behalf to move in wisdom and concern about what is best for *them*.

For instance, in some circumstances, it may be best for the children to only have supervised visits with their father. However, there is a vast difference between saying, "In order to keep everyone safe, Daddy will have a friend hang out with you guys. If you feel uncomfortable, you can use your words with all the adults," versus, "Your dad is such a loser, and I don't even want you to see him. But I have to, and I hate it! I bet you do too." You may very well feel that way, and I understand it. But it is your job as a parent to learn what language and attitude supports the well-being of your children.

The question, "What is best for the kids?" is my rubric for every decision regarding co-parenting. It is my Northern star when I am faced with any decision. Sure, it may feel good for me to roll my eyes, or vent when I'm frustrated, but any criticism I make against my children's father is internalized by them, as if I am criticizing a part of *them*. If I tried to hurt their connection to him, I would be hurting them. A child's attachment and self-concept are tightly knit with both parents, regardless of the quality of character of the parents. It was important for me to realize that my kids' attachment to their dad was important to their mental and emotional health. Once I learned that, I did everything I could to be positive and encouraging of that attachment. When they missed him, I encouraged them to call him. When they were angry about the divorce, I validated their feelings without blasting their dad. When they brought up something fun they did with their dad and his girlfriend, I celebrated with them. In those early days, it was excruciating and nauseating, but I knew that the price for our brokenness was not something I wanted my children to pay. If it had to be hard, and it often was, I wanted it to be hard for *me*, not them.

I am not encouraging you to lie on your ex's behalf or pretend like everything is okay when it is clearly not. When my children had questions, I answered with age-appropriate honesty that still honored their dad's role in their lives. It is not easy; these conversations often catch me off guard, and I rely on the Holy Spirit to guide me. He has been so faithful to give me the words when I need them, and to convict me when I misspeak. It is always a reality check when these conversations come from left field, because as Jesus made clear, "What you say flows from what is in your heart" (Luke 6:45). Like a full pitcher that gets bumped unexpectedly, I find that what spills from my mouth during these unforeseen conversations is a good indicator of how my healing and forgiveness journey is progressing. Knowing that my heart posture is going to be affecting my children is a great motivator to keep seeking the Lord to help me walk in love.

I remember one conversation when my oldest was about five years old:

> "Mom, I miss Daddy. I don't like divorce."
>
> "I know, honey. You love your daddy and he loves you. Divorce is bad, and it hurts everyone in the family. It's okay to be sad."
>
> "Did you want the divorce, Mommy?"
>
> "No, honey. It makes me sad too, but God helps my heart."
>
> "Did Daddy want the divorce? Even though it's bad?"

My heart stopped. If I said no, I would be lying. He *did* make a bad choice, and I could not excuse it. But I had an opportunity to show a godly response to sin.

"Yes, baby. He did not want to be married anymore, and that was a choice that hurt all of us, including him. But we forgive people when they make bad choices, and we pray for God to heal us. Let's pray for us, and for Daddy."

These conversations always feel intense and important, and they are. The standard of "what is best for the kids" has never steered me wrong. Even when I don't quite get it right the first time, God has always given me wisdom and grace to communicate with my children what they need. Above all, I am teaching them to bring their questions and pain to the Lord and to let Him hold us as we heal.

Even after the divorce is finalized and you have fully accepted the end of the marriage, there is a continuous journey of hope and grief regarding your children's relationship with their other parent, and the effects of the divorce on their life. Seek God at every turn, and He will equip you to be your child's guide on that journey. As you model forgiveness, grace, dignity, and dependence on the Lord, your children will draw strength from you as they cope with their new reality. God is faithful to you, and He will be faithful to them.

PRAYER

God, thank You for walking this road with me and covering me with Your grace. Divorce was not my desire when I got married, but it is my reality now, and I invite You into it with me. Show me how to operate in this new type of relationship with my ex. Give me wisdom on where my boundaries need to be. Fill me with Your Spirit and Your strength.

APPLICATION

1. What is one 'password' you need to change?

2. Give an example of how you have been a great ex. What is something you could work on to be a better ex?

3. If you have children, how does the question, "What is best for the kids?" challenge some of your attitudes and decisions?

She is not Perfection

It is easy
To believe
The lie

Is her skin smooth where mine is scarred?
Her body thinner?
Her laugh more joyful?
Her touch more kind?
Her gaze more piercing?

Maybe she had the right curves
Maybe she wasn't afraid of heights
Maybe she found the perfect words

The ones I fumbled over
The ones that convinced him to leave...
...or maybe not

She is not Evil

It is easy
To believe
The lie

Is her moral compass south where mine is north?
Is she filth and I am pure?

Is she a monster?
Is she worthless?
Worth less than me?

Maybe she is incapable of real love
Maybe she will forever wreck homes and never build one
Maybe she will break his heart

The one I treasured for years
The one I nearly died trying to save…
…or maybe not

She is a Woman

As am I

She is a Daughter

Wounded, gifted, flawed and lovely
Capable of harming
Or helping

As am I

She is not the enemy
The L<small>IES</small> are the enemy
The ones that whisper in her ears
And in mine

The ones that say we are not enough
That we need to
Look that way
Own that thing
Reach that status
Have that man
In order to be
What we already are

Oh, how the lies rob us

Her dignity
My honor

They are connected

Woven together
It sears me
But it is true

To be free
I release us both to wellness

To be whole
I bless us both to health

To be loved
I proclaim both of our beauty

So no—
I do not fear her
She is not better

And no—
I do not hate her
She is not worse

She's my Sister
Forgiven and loved
Whether she slays and steals
Or repents and restores
My heart must stay the course

Father, forgive them
They know not what they do

10

FORGIVENESS

FINDING FREEDOM IN RELEASE

The depth of this wound is beyond words, and it reaches into every corner of your heart and mind. Forgiving your husband and his mistress for the affair may feel impossible. How can anyone forgive something this awful? There is no doubt, adultery is inexcusable, unacceptable—but is it unforgivable?

We must once again return to God's Word, for our hearts and minds are not wise enough to guide us well on our own; we need our Creator to lead us into truth and light. Even when it seems impossible or feels too hard, we can trust God to not only show us the way to walk in, but to carry us through.

FOR YOUR GOOD

Before we explore the *what's* and *how-to's* of forgiveness, I must stress how important choosing to forgive is for the health of your own heart.

We all know of someone who is bitter and resentful over something that happened years ago. When they tell their story, they seem like they are right back there, living it. When you think of them, do you admire that about them? Or aspire to be where they are? I'm confident that you want better—that you're longing for a much higher level of healing and happiness. And I'm even more confident that God has better for you! That's why He calls you to forgive, because He knows how unsafe and damaging it will be to you to hold on to this hurt.

Unforgiveness is like seeing that someone set your house on fire and blocking the door from the inside so they can't get out. You're trying to make sure they get punished for what they have done, but *you* will also get burned if you stay in the building. They may have climbed out the window, but you're still in there, covered in smoke and flames. Get out, sister! The damage is done to the house, but it's your choice if you let it continue to damage you. God is calling you out into the fresh air.

One of the reasons we're often resistant to leaving the smoke and flames behind is we want justice for the wrong done to us by our husband—we don't want him to get away with it! He won't, believe me. Our God's justice is sure and strong. Remember what His Word says about the path that your husband is on: destruction, bondage, death. Either the punishment of these sins will fall on his shoulders in due time, or he will cry out to Jesus, and Jesus will pay the debt. Either way, this evil will be dealt with by natural consequences and by your righteous and protective Father. You can trust Him to be the Judge.

It's so much easier said than done, I know. You've been through so much, and I know it can feel unbearable. Forgiveness can feel unfair. I remember the day I wrestled with God about this.

"God, I know you want me to forgive him. But how? What he is doing is SO WRONG."

*It **is** so wrong, Ruthie. I know, honey.*

"I don't think I can do this. It hurts so badly. I need Your help. Show me how."

Come with Me. Let Me show you something.

He led me to the cross. My sweet Jesus, suffering and dying, broken and bleeding—for me. My heart broke to see Him humiliated, alone, and hurting like that. I had been here before, at His feet, but it struck my heart afresh. I could never get used to seeing this. I could never get over the sacrifice He made for me. Tears streamed down my face, as I looked again at the Holy One. His blood purchased me, saved me, brought me close to the Father.

"Jesus, I love You. Thank You for loving me this much."

Look closer, now, honey. What do you see?

I saw Jesus' blood, dripping from His fingers. From these hands that formed the world, that calmed the storms, that wiped my tears. The blood flowed down, precious and holy.

Then I saw him. My husband, face down at the cross. I saw her, too, weeping at the feet of Jesus.

You know My blood is enough for you. Thank you for trusting Me with your heart, Ruthie. Is My blood enough for them?

My knees buckled as I fell to the floor, wailing in worship. How could I deny Him? For all the pain these sins cost me, they cost Jesus more. Who was I to tell Him it wasn't enough? That I needed more? No. Worthy is the Lamb that was slain, to receive the *full* reward of His suffering. The blood that purchased my forgiveness also purchased theirs, and to deny God's forgiveness of them would be to reject His forgiveness of me. If I was to receive the full blessing of God's sacrifice and forgiveness, I had to accept that it covers me *and* those that hurt me. His blood was more than enough.

As I began to walk in forgiveness, I felt lighter, cleaner, closer to Jesus. Forgiveness is a decision, but it is more than that; it is a posture of the heart. Every time a new injury was inflicted upon me, I had to choose to return to this posture of forgiveness, and years later, I still adopt this position towards those who hurt me. While there were and are moments when this is breathtakingly challenging, it has always been worth it.

One of the things that has helped me to avoid the dangers of bitterness and to keep choosing this posture, is understanding what forgiveness is and is not. Failing to correctly understand what God is asking of us can be a stumbling block that keeps us from walking in the freedom and wholeness that God provides.

WHAT FORGIVENESS IS NOT

Forgiveness is not permission to sin. It is not shifting the responsibility off of the offender. It is not removing consequences. It is not minimizing the damage, or excusing the behavior. Forgiveness does not say it's not a big deal, or what happened was okay. Forgiveness is not denial. It does not trivialize pain and suffering.

Forgiveness does not mean forgetting. God is able to forget our sins (e.g., Psalm 103:12, Isaiah 43:25), but our human minds are limited, and nowhere in Scripture does it teach that forgiveness requires us to forget. Years after the affair, I remember, in vivid detail, so many things about it and the lies and abuse it brought into my life. But while I still remember, forgiveness has brought healing so that those memories no longer have the power to injure me. I am safe and released from the sting, only because of the work that forgiveness has done in my heart, not because I have forgotten.

Forgiveness is not emotional detachment. There is a common misconception that if you have strong feelings, especially of anger, that you are not walking in forgiveness. While we must guard ourselves from staying angry for too long, it is important to realize that anger itself is not a sin. We are commanded to not sin in our anger (Ephesians 4:26), but we are not commanded to remain anger-free. God Himself expresses righteous anger all throughout Scripture, and we see also that Jesus experienced anger towards the people He came to forgive while grieving for them *at the same time*. When the Pharisees were trying to trap and accuse Jesus,

"He looked around at them with anger, grieved at their hardness of heart" (Mark 3:5, ESV). You can walk in forgiveness while experiencing the full range of God-given emotions that come from being violated and wronged.

Forgiveness is not the same thing as reconciliation. Reconciliation requires trust, which is a two-way street. In order for trust to be re-established, your husband has to earn it. Once trust is broken, it must be rebuilt, and the majority of the responsibility for that process is on him. Reconciliation has requirements. Confession, godly sorrow and the *fruit of repentance* (Matthew 3:8) are all needed to lay the ground for reconciliation. In Matthew 18, Jesus instructs His disciples on how to deal with the sin of another Christian:

> *"If your brother or sister sins, go and point out their fault, just between the two of you. If they listen to you, you have won them over. But if they will not listen, take one or two others along, so that 'every matter may be established by the testimony of two or three witnesses.' If they still refuse to listen, tell it to the church; and if they refuse to listen even to the church,* **treat them as you would a pagan or a tax collector.***"*
>
> *Matthew 18:15-17 (NIV, emphasis mine)*

This process is necessary to repair the breech of relationship caused by sin, but the outcome clearly depends on the choices of the perpetrator. Keep in mind that elsewhere in Scripture, God instructs His people to not be unequally yoked in marriage with unbelievers (2 Corinthians 6:14), and that if an unbeliever leaves their spouse, the bereft spouse is not enslaved to their vows, but called to peace by God (1 Corinthians 7:15). So, if your spouse is unrepentant, and therefore should be considered an unbeliever, reconciliation is not at all a requirement.

Forgiveness, on the other hand, does not have the same limitations as reconciliation. You can forgive someone even if they are not sorry. Forgiveness is not earned, it is given. It is an expensive and painful gift, but it is not just one that you give to the one who hurt you. *It is also a gift to yourself.* The alternative to forgiveness is unforgiveness, which is a sin. Unforgiveness will only separate you from God, your source of healing.

WHAT FORGIVENESS IS

Forgiveness is faith. Forgiveness is faith that the blood of Jesus is sufficient to cover *every* sin, even the ones that are committed against you. Forgiveness acknowledges the enormity of the hurt, the full depravity of the sin, and boldly confesses that Jesus' blood is enough to cover even this. If it cost nothing, there would be no need for this faith, no need for a belief in God to accomplish this. But the bigger the hurt, the more honor is given to Jesus for covering the sin.

Forgiveness is faith that the justice of God is sufficient. It admits that God doesn't need our help in assigning judgement. We have nothing to add to His perfect justice. Forgiveness is a declaration of trust that God will handle what we cannot. We long for justice, and can trust that God will make everything right in every way. Forgiveness requires that we surrender that process to the One who is worthy, trusting that His timing and His decisions regarding justice are better than ours, and beyond our ability to understand.

Forgiveness is faith that what God says is true. We forgive if for no other reason than to demonstrate our obedience to and trust in God's Word. The world says, "You have every right to withhold forgiveness." But Jesus says, "If you refuse to forgive others, your Father will not forgive your sins" (Matthew 6:15). He is repeatedly clear that if we want to receive forgiveness from the Father, we must first be willing to forgive those who have wronged us (Mark 11:25).

Some people think this is a harsh requirement, but this hammer of truth is here to break off the chains the enemy is trying to lock you in. And when we consider Who said them, we know that He has every right to ask us to forgive. Jesus never sinned, and no one has ever needed to forgive Him, and yet as He hung innocent upon the cross, He chose a path of forgiveness (Luke 23:34). I am committed to following Jesus. If He asks me to forgive, I will do it, if for no other reason than it is what He wants. Thankfully, there are even more blessings that come with forgiveness. In His ways are true life, and we can have full faith that His way is the best for us.

Forgiveness is freedom. Forgiveness is freedom from the weight of judgement that you are not built to carry. Sin needs to be judged, but hearts do not need to be judged by you—that right and responsibility belongs to God alone. Remember, He sees everything and He loves you. He hates the wickedness that has entered into your life, and He is protective of you. He always strikes the perfect balance of judgement and mercy, and you can trust Him. We cannot always trust ourselves to be fair, wise, and righteous, but He frees us from that burden. The Scriptures call us to let Him carry that weight, exhorting us not to try and get justice for ourselves, but to "Wait for the Lord to handle the matter" (Proverbs 20:22).

God is not asking you to forgive so that this grievous sin can be glossed over or minimized. God will bring justice. He is, however, asking that you leave it in His capable hands to deal with. Paul was loving but firm with the early Church on this matter, instructing them, "Beloved, never avenge yourselves, but leave it to the wrath of God, for it is written, 'Vengeance is mine, I will repay, says the Lord'" (Romans 12:19, ESV). Revenge is tempting, but it is a trap. None of us is qualified or deserving to take God's place. It's too heavy. It will crush you. Let Him have it, and be free from the weight of it.

Forgiveness is freedom from bitterness and envy that will rot you from the inside. You may have heard the saying that unforgiveness is like drinking poison and hoping the other person dies. That poison is bitterness. Scripture is full of instruction to avoid bitterness and envy. I encourage you to read Psalm 37 and Psalm 73 in their entirety. You will be relieved to find that you are not alone in your strong feelings, and that God has His ways of bringing justice to wickedness. You will also discover why you do not want to get trapped in the snare of unforgiveness and bitterness. Such things cause further trouble, defiling us, and blocking the flow of God's grace in our lives (Hebrews 12:15).

Sister, we need all the grace we can get! Especially in this time, you do not want to add to your trouble, or separate yourself from God's grace, which will sustain you. Trust Him to deal with the sin and injustice, keep your heart clean so you can welcome healing in. Proverbs 14:30 reminds us: "A healed heart is life to the flesh, and rottenness to the bones is envy" (YLT). A healed heart is what you want—you want the life-giving flow of a heart that has been made whole through the riches of His grace!

Forgiveness brings freedom from soul ties that will torment and bind you. Whenever you hold something against someone it means you cannot hold more life-giving things. That thing you hold against them bears weight and takes up space in your hands. It also connects you. In order to hold it against them, you have to stay close and focused on them and their movements. Unforgiveness binds you close to someone else, and that heart tie can pull you around. As long as you are tied together with someone through unforgiveness, their actions and opinion of you affect you deeply. You actually give them power over your mood and your thought life. But forgiveness releases you from these unhealthy connections, and allows you to maintain greater ownership of your heart and mind. It also frees you up to hold what is good. As long as there is unforgiveness in your heart, that internal real estate cannot be used for love. But once forgiveness is given, all that space is open to be filled back up with better things.

Forgiveness is fullness. As the barriers of offense and bitterness come down, you are open to receive the full measure of God's love; unhindered by any walls it can flow freely to you and through you. You may not even realize it, but if you hold unforgiveness in your heart against a person, it actually disconnects you from other people and the Lord. Once those walls are gone, you can experience deeper intimacy with God than you ever thought possible.

Forgiving others opens up the fullness of God's forgiveness over your own life. When you choose to forgive, you are participating with Christ, experiencing something that He died to do. I never understood how much it cost Jesus to forgive me until I had to forgive someone else. Even then, I have only had a glimpse into the price He paid. I became aware of how many times I had overlooked God, or chosen to spend my time, energy, affection, worship on something else, giving Him less than He deserves. Forgiving my husband helped me see how much God loves and forgives *me*.

Forgiveness also brings us into the fullness of God's presence. Because forgiveness is God-created, and divine, it gives us more connection to Him. I could never forgive in my own strength; I had to be hidden in Christ to do it (Colossians 3:3). Connecting myself to Him like that was the most intimate thing I could have imagined with Jesus. Walking out the road that He was leading me on, participating in His suffering love, and having a small understanding of what carrying my cross with Him meant, drew me close to Him. That nearness and dependence on His heart brought so much blessing and light into my own.

I hope you see the value and power of forgiveness, and that you are ready to press deeper into this holy work. It is important for your wholeness that you forgive everyone involved. I know how daunting that sounds, but together we will walk through some practical ways to activate forgiveness.

FORGIVING YOUR HUSBAND

Your husband is the primary offender in this situation, and therefore, the majority of your forgiveness will be directed towards him. Whether reconciliation with your husband happens or not, forgiving him is critical for *your* healing. It is also necessary obedience to the Lord. Remember, even if there is no repentance, God will honor your submission and surrender to Himself. Regardless of any response you receive, you will experience the power of God's Spirit working in and through you.

Forgiving your husband will likely be an exercise you have to continually repeat. For me, every time I found out a new detail I didn't know before, or he did something new that was hurtful and offensive, I had to forgive again. There will be layers of hurt, waves of wounds, that your forgiveness will meet over time. Do not be discouraged that you did not 'get it all' at once—you are not doing it wrong. Forgiveness is like a muscle that, when exercised regularly, becomes strong and second nature to use over a long span of time.

Many of the women I have coached have become discouraged when, after months of working towards healing, they find themselves needing to forgive *again*. I want to remind you, just as I remind them, that forgiveness is not a one-time accomplishment. I like to think of it as a place in which I live. I live in forgiveness because I am hidden in Christ. I picture myself wrapped up in Jesus, covered by everything He is and carries. When you live in forgiveness, offenses and surges of feeling may come to visit, but you choose whether or not to let them move you out of forgiveness, or to let them pass through while you stay planted firmly in Jesus. If you are ever swept away and find yourself outside of that forgiving posture, do not fear; it is not too late to let Jesus bring you back in.

Deciding to start the journey of forgiving your husband is a huge step, but there is grace to cover you. If you feel like you are unable to forgive, invite Jesus into the process and let Him help you. Seek prayer from those you trust. You do not have to do this alone.

FORGIVING THE OTHER WOMAN

It takes strength and love to forgive the woman who has been with your husband. You may feel like you do not have what you need, but thankfully, strength and love are things that Jesus can give you. Refusing to forgive her will create a strong tie between your life and hers, and it will actually give her power to continue hurting and shaming you, even if she doesn't know you. Releasing her into forgiveness will enable you to continue to heal and stand with dignity.

When I forgave the woman my husband was cheating on me with, the scales fell off my eyes and I could see more clearly. I still had pangs of jealousy and moments of insecurity, but the power was gone once I determined to live out forgiveness. It shocked my husband. I remember looking at him straight in the eyes and saying, "She deserves to be more than some dirty little secret. No woman deserves that. You should marry her and make an honest woman out of her." He could not believe I was saying that, and honestly, I had a hard time believing it too. God's Spirit was speaking truth through me. There were many other choice words I could have said about her in my flesh, but I remembered what God had shown me about her. She was guilty, she was broken, she was wrong—but she was not my enemy. My struggle was not truly against her, "but against the rulers, against the powers, against the world forces of this darkness, against the spiritual forces of wickedness in the heavenly places" (Ephesians 6:12, NASB).

The same evil that was tormenting her was trying to attach itself to me. It is trying to attach itself to you, too. The forces of darkness want you to stay insecure and bitter, by having you come into agreement with the lie that she is better or worse than you. Do not empower this darkness, but crush it with forgiveness. The truth is that you are both daughters of God, both created by Him for love—a love that neither of you are receiving. She is receiving lust and perversion; you are receiving betrayal and abandonment. She is trespassing in a sacred place that God had designed for you alone and there will be consequences for that choice, but it is not your place to enforce them. She has been given permission from your husband, and it was his responsibility to protect you, not hers. It was his vow to love you, not hers. As you forgive her, you release her into the hands of a righteous and holy God. She will choose to repent and receive grace and freedom, or she will choose to reject God and continue walking in darkness towards death.

In the early days, my body would send a surge of adrenaline at the thought of her or the mention of her name. But I began to turn to Jesus each time and ask for His help to keep this posture of forgiveness. Shortly after the separation, my children were introduced to her by their dad and they had a relationship with her. They of course had no understanding of who she was to me and would ask to pray for her with me before bedtime, because they knew she did not know Jesus. At first it knocked the wind out of me to hear her name in their mouths. But by God's grace, I was able to pray with them for her. Eventually I meant every word. "Jesus, bless her. Bring her to You. Help my children show her Your love. Amen."

I knew that God had worked a miracle of forgiveness in my heart when I began pleading for her salvation in my own prayers. Eventually I did not want punishment for her, I wanted mercy.

You may feel so far from that place. Sister, do not be discouraged. I did not start there. You do not have to be any further than you are today. Take this one step at a time and let Jesus do the heavy lifting. When you cannot bear the anger, disgust, and judgement, talk to Him about it. Give it to Him. I promise you, He is faithful to listen to you, carry the weight, and give you the strength to let it go.

RECEIVE FORGIVENESS FOR YOURSELF

I hope I have been clear that you are not in any way, under any circumstances, responsible for the affair. There is nothing you have done or not done that has forced your husband to be unfaithful to you. Nothing. It was not your fault, and you do not need to apologize for the adultery. It is not your sin, and you did not break the covenant.

However, I know that for myself, I had plenty of things *inside* of my marriage that I did imperfectly. After my husband told me he didn't love me anymore, but before I found out about the affair, I did a long inventory of my weaknesses. I spent a week making a list of things that I needed to work on and repent of. Unfortunately, when I brought it to him, I was met with hostility and indifference. He did not accept my apologies, and told me he thought I could never change. With hindsight, I can see that he was capitalizing on my vulnerability and manipulating it to cover his tracks. However, there was still good for me that came out of being honest and humble enough to admit my faults. God honored my heart and brought fruit out of my efforts, and healing through His forgiveness of me.

I am not suggesting that you take a list of your weaknesses to your husband right now. It's likely not a safe time for you to be emotionally vulnerable like that. If your marriage does survive, there will be a time when you can and should share those things with him, but please make sure you are well into recovery, with a solid support system before you open up your heart. If your marriage does not survive, you still may want to repent of things at some point, but again, please wait until you have reached a place in your healing that this cannot be an effective weapon if turned against you.

Regardless of the state of your connection to your husband, an honest assessment of yourself is always healthy. You want your heart to be whole, and the cleansing and healing that happens with repentance and confession are powerful. The apostle John tells us that, "If we confess our sins, he is faithful and just to forgive us our sins and to cleanse us from all unrighteousness" (1 John 1:9, ESV). And in James we read that for us to be healed, it is necessary to confess our sins to each other and pray for one another. He also reminds us that "The earnest prayer of a righteous person has great power and produces wonderful results" (James 5:16). Scripture teaches that confession leads us into righteousness, which not only connects us more to God's heart, but also makes our prayers more effective and opens up healing over our lives. I know it can be intimidating and vulnerable, but clearing your conscience with both God and other believers will do wonders for your heart as you walk through this season.

Taking responsibility for your own sins and failures is an important step towards more freedom. But you also need to accept God's forgiveness of you. I have seen too many women hold onto guilt and shame, nurturing it and empowering it as it robs them of joy and peace. No matter what you have done, Jesus' blood is enough to cover it. Let Him wrap His robe of righteousness around you, as you allow His forgiveness to wash over you.

PRAYER

God, forgiving in my own strength is too much for me. The hurt runs too deep for me to do this on my own. Thank You for paving the way for me and offering me Your forgiveness first. Help me accept Your forgiveness and trust that it will flow to me, through me, and out of me. Thank You for Your justice and mercy. I trust You to cover everything that I cannot reach. Teach me to take one moment at a time, and to follow You step by step on this journey.

APPLICATION

1. What is the most difficult thing for you to believe about forgiveness?

2. If you have had a lack of forgiveness, what has that cost you? If you've been walking in forgiveness, what has that given you?

3. Think back on your marriage. Are there any unconfessed sins, or patterns of behavior that you had that you did not take responsibility for? Take some time to write them out, and ask God to forgive you for each.

(Please visit the appendix at the end of this book for an extended application on forgiveness.)

Thanks:
   Strange
   Sideways
   Gratitude

Thorn removed
Weight lifted
No longer
Held
Under
Water

Amputation:
   Cruel
   Kind
   Removal

Killed the limb
Saved the body,
The soul,
Me

Goodbye:
   Bitter
   Sweet
   Return

I remain,
Flourishing
Breath and blood
Circulating
To healthy
Parts

Blessing:
  Well-wish
  Eulogy
  Benediction

Be whole
And free
And gone

I will miss
Nothing that
Is
No
Longer

And savor
Everything that
Once
Really
Was

And crave
All that
Awaits
My
Reborn
Heart

11

GRIEF

BEING PRESENT IN THE PROCESS

Grieving is the painful process of carrying a hurt or loss into a place of acceptance. Every person's process has a different pace, style, and progression. There is no formula for grief, or rule book to follow. Many of us have heard about the five stages of grief developed by Elisabeth Kübler-Ross in her book, "On Death and Dying," and may think that these stages—denial, anger, bargaining, depression, and acceptance—are linear and universal. However, this theory of grief was primarily anecdotal, and Kübler-Ross herself posed that not everyone experiences these stages in this particular order, and that some do not experience every stage. Grief seems to be as unique as the individuals experiencing it and can be unpredictable.

There are no hard and fast rules about how you should grieve, and while this can leave you feeling confused and alone, unsure of whether you are doing this 'right', it also means that there is great freedom. There is no one right way to grieve, sister, there is just an honest way—*your way*.

HONEST AND FREE

This may be the first major grief you have experienced in your life, and you may not know what to expect from yourself. Or maybe you have walked through grief before, but this feels different because it is not just loss, it is also a violation. As I have coached women through their grief, I've found one of the most important things you can do is to give yourself full permission to feel your feelings as they come. It doesn't matter what order they come in, or with what intensity, just allow yourself to be present to them without rushing them on. As you experience all these different emotions, try to stay curious rather than judgmental of yourself. Because the emotions can be so powerful and seem to overtake us, I find it helpful to look at them like large visitors, taking up space in my inner world. I can welcome them, say hello, listen to what they have to say, knowing that they will not stay forever.

"Hello, Anger. Take a seat. Tell me about why you're here today."

I am not anger. I am *feeling* anger. I am responsible for my choices, and for what I do with what my anger is telling me, but the feeling itself does not define me. It is a neutral party. I accept its presence, learn what I can, and release it to go. For instance, one thing I learned from anger is that it not only sends me a signal that something is wrong, but it also carries a power to move me into a safer space. Anger helped me to summon the courage to put up boundaries, energizing me to take necessary action to try to rescue my marriage and ultimately to rescue myself. This visitor had something important to say, and I am glad that I did not lock it out of my heart. That said, just like any other visitor, if I had locked it in the basement and not allowed it to leave, it would have caused major problems.

So many people fear being trapped with their feelings, but I assure you, if you leave the door open for them to come and go, they will pass. As we engage with them, we will be able to harvest all the necessary good that they bring while knowing that we will not have to live with them forever. Allowing them space is the only way to walk in honesty about where we are and how we are really feeling.

Whether you are grieving the loss of your marriage and husband, or you are reconciling yet grieving the loss of trust and time, be determined to stay real about it. Some outsiders may not be comfortable seeing something so raw and honest inside of you. There may be relationships that require different boundaries in order to stay healthy. I love how Brené Brown defines a boundary as, "The closest distance in which I can love both you *and* me." This means boundaries are not about rejection, they are about love.

If being close to your grief causes someone to be too uncomfortable to stay close, I assure you, that is no reason to shut yourself down. That relationship might need a little more distance, but you deserve to find relationships in which you can be honest and free about your grief.

Because many people may not know how to handle their own grief, or yours, it will be important for you to communicate as clearly as you can about what you need. I know that may seem overwhelming, especially when the roller-coaster of grief causes your needs to shift rapidly. It is okay for you to change your mind about what is helpful at this time, just remember that people cannot know what you are thinking, and while it is not your responsibility to manage someone else's responses or reactions to your grief, it is your responsibility to communicate if you need something to change. I know it is difficult, and it may seem unfair to have to spend energy doing that hard work, but you deserve the best support you can get. It is likely that there are many people in your life who truly want to be supportive and helpful—draw strength from those people by teaching them how they can love you well. One day it may be conversation. The next day it may be space. That is okay, sister. Remember, there's no right way to grieve, just your way.

WILD GRIEF

Depending on what culture you were raised in, you may feel pressure to contain your grief to something quiet, controlled, and private. However, I want to encourage you to be open to the possibility that your heart and your actual body may need to process your pain with greater abandon.

God created our bodies to heal themselves. I know there are limits to this, but consider how complex and amazing our immune system is: When we are sick, our bodies respond with symptoms that are unpleasant—miserable even. Yet those same symptoms are how our body fights to restore our health; we are designed to partner with restoration. In a similar way, God designed grief to be a healing process for our hearts, souls, and even our bodies.

In many cultures it is socially acceptable to express grief in very demonstrative ways, and women, in particular, can be expected to wail loudly for days at a time. However, in more stoic cultures, people may not feel permission to 'go there'. While there is certainly room for different cultural expressions, a survey of Scripture provides us with insight about how God feels about displaying grief. Not only are there numerous instances where God's people wailed and wept corporately (e.g., Esther 4:3, Mark 5:38), pounded their chests (Luke 18:13), and ripped their clothing in grief (2 Samuel 1:1-11), but God Himself weeps and instructs His people to call for mourning and wailing (Jeremiah 9). Jesus also wept at the tomb of His friend, Lazarus (John 11:35), and cried out in anguish, sweating profusely in the garden of Gethsemane before He was betrayed (Luke 22:44).

Grief can get loud and wild. I know mine did. My most unbridled expressions of pain were helpful in getting the anguish out of my body. I screamed, I wailed, I pounded the floor, I pulled at my hair. While I urge you to make sure you remain physically safe, I offer you permission to get as wild as you need to release the agony. It is biblical.

One instance of wild grief is vivid in my memory. It was towards the end of my ninety-day waiting period that I had set with the Lord, and my husband was still unrepentant. I started walking around the house, pacing and praying.

"God, I can't do this anymore. Please give me strength to keep holding on or give me the strength to let go."

Oh, Ruthie. I'm so proud of you. You've held on long enough, baby girl. It's time to let him go.

"I want to… but how can I? He's so deceived, and I don't want to abandon him, even after everything he's done."

I will never leave him. I will chase him every moment he has breath in his body.

"I promised to love him unconditionally. Like You love, God. I don't want to do the wrong thing."

You loved well. Your covenant was broken. You must forgive him, and love him as My child, but you are released from loving him as your husband. He released you. I asked you to wait, but now I release you.

"Lord, I want to be free. But I also want to be like You. If You want me to lay down my life for him, I'll keep doing it. Even if it kills me. It killed You. Your love has no boundaries!"

Even My love has boundaries, Ruthie. A man has his lifetime to turn to Me, but no longer. If My perfect love leaves the door open for only a time, yours should too. You left the door open long enough. It's time to close it and go. There is only death here, and I created you for life.

My knees buckled, and the cool linoleum of my kitchen floor greeted my surrender. I had gone from fighting my husband, to fighting for him, but there was no more fight in me. It was time to accept that he was gone—for good.

I wept and wailed as though I had just heard the news of his death. His life and our love flashed through my mind. I saw him, as he truly was, in his purest form, and I loved him. He shone bright, and his smile beamed. He was laughing, with his head thrown back— my favorite sound. But then he started to fade and wither away. Darkness crowded in, and he became smaller. The light dulled, and the laughter echoed for the last time. The man I knew and loved was gone. He was gone. He had fallen into an abyss I could not reach. It was as though I had seen him for the last time. The sum of him, everything I loved, tied up together, was worthy of my grief.

My forehead gently bounced off the floor and my palms smacked the ground as I rocked back and forth, screaming his name.

My despair was fresh, but it was clean. I was saying goodbye to my best friend and my lover, without the stain of bitterness or betrayal. I honored him with the grief of a widow. With every breath, every scream, my body bid him farewell. Each time my forehead met the kitchen floor, the rhythm of grief washed over me like a wave. I felt connected to the pain of every woman who had ever wailed over her dead.

"NOOOOOOO!!"

My agony this time was for him, not for myself. I interceded for him; my whole body was a prayer. *Jesus, help him! Save him!* I knew what was at stake. His very soul, precious and beautiful, was being warred over. Such a deep darkness had invaded him, and the torment broke my heart for him. If only I could stop it! I would have given anything to free him. Yet even as I wailed, I could feel myself being lifted out of the battlefield. Every breath, powerful and guttural, propelled me away. Eventually I sensed God's Spirit place me gently in a safe and soft place. I was sprawled out and spent, but the kitchen floor became a pool of peace, as my breathing slowed, and my screams turned to whimpers. Jesus held me close, and I knew I was going to be okay.

While that memorable day was a turning point for me, this would not be the last wave of grief that would overtake me. Some were wild, like this one, and other waves required a different response. Grief ebbs and flows, like water in the ocean. One day I would feel strong and steady, with the grief lapping gently at my feet. The next I would be engulfed by a huge wave, carrying the full weight and intensity of my hurt and loss. It was never predictable, but over time,

I learned how to let the grief wash over me without fighting it. I began to notice that the waves were spread out further and further, and I had more days of peace. As I allowed the work of grief to be accomplished in my life, without resisting or running from it, I became grateful for the unexpected treasure that it brought me.

THE GIFT OF GRIEF

Grief has the capacity to open and enlarge our hearts. It's a painful process, and yet if we tune into the deepest parts of ourselves, we can appreciate that our hearts were meant to be this big.

Scripture talks about this enlarging through pain:

> *All around us we observe a pregnant creation. The difficult times of pain throughout the world are simply birth pangs. But it's not only around us; it's within us. The Spirit of God is arousing us within. We're also feeling the birth pangs. These sterile and barren bodies of ours are yearning for full deliverance. That is why waiting does not diminish us, any more than waiting diminishes a pregnant mother.* **We are enlarged in the waiting.** *We, of course, don't see what is enlarging us. But the longer we wait, the larger we become, and the more joyful our expectancy.*
>
> Romans 8:24-25 (MSG, emphasis mine)

As I waited, I expanded. As the waves of pain came, like contractions during labor, I leaned in, allowing it to do its work. I could not see what was being birthed in my life, and I certainly had not asked for or expected this process. But just as in birth, when a woman can work *with* the contractions, accepting and leaning into each one, there is a beautiful surrender that allows the power inside her to do something we would normally think of as impossible. A strength and resilience was forged inside of me as I labored through my grief. As I clung to truth and God's Spirit, the waves that once appeared like they were drowning me began to wash me. The water began to smooth jagged edges, like sea glass in the sand, worn down into something beautiful. My grief was a gift.

It may seem crazy to see grief as a gift. No one wants to suffer. No one enjoys loss. We are bent to resist pain, to find a way out, to seek comfort. Remember, even Jesus prayed to have the cup taken from Him (Matthew 26:39).

Yet there is a great mystery in grief. There are truths we cannot know until we are scraped to our rawest, most riveted parts. There are beauties we cannot see until our eyes are filled with tears. There are depths of love we cannot know until our hearts have been broken and resurrections we cannot witness until the dying comes. If we are brave enough to turn to God in the process, grief can introduce us to new aspects of who God is. I never knew God as my strong tower, my refuge, until I needed a place to hide. I never knew God as my rescuer, my deliverer, until I was placed in a terrible battle. I never knew God as my healer until I was deeply wounded. He is my comforter, my redeemer, my rock, the lifter of my head—and my grief was the painful pathway to meeting these beautiful parts of Him.

Grief can introduce us to a part of ourselves we may have never wanted to know. I never wanted to know if I was strong enough to endure a tragedy like this. But here I was, surviving and strengthened under a weight I did not ask for. My innermost parts were tested. My faith grew and firmed up in the face of my greatest fear, and my capacity for grace and forgiveness was expanded. I could hardly believe how fiercely beautiful I became in the middle of the fire. God's Spirit filled and transformed me, while my obedience and surrender in the middle of my grief proved to me that I could be trusted to carry God's presence. What a gift to meet the warrior priestess God had created me to be.

I also discovered the ways that grief can introduce us to each other in new and deepened ways. My friendships went to a different level, as I opened myself up to safe people in the middle of my grief. Their fingerprints were all over the shaping and healing I was going through. The connection that was built in these relationships never could have happened without the vulnerability and intensity grief brought me.

Grief is a gift no one asks for, but it is a gift, nonetheless. But while it is a gift, it is also not a state that God intends us to stay in indefinitely. He is after all, the God who turns mourning into dancing (Psalm 30:11), and so there must come a time where we allow our grief to settle and look to the new things that God has for us.

FINDING CLOSURE

Every grief needs closure. Sometimes closure just takes time, and more time. But more often than not, when we make a marker in time with some sort of intention, it can bring a big deposit of resolution. It is as though the map of our lives, what helps us make sense of our stories, needs mile-markers to help us articulate where we have been.

Most of our big events in life are marked with some sort of ceremony or rite of passage. Birthdays have parties, graduates have convocation, pregnant mothers have showers, bereft families have burials. This big life event, your marriage breaking, deserves a ceremony. There are no rules about what you should do, or when—everyone's path of grieving moves in different patterns, at different paces. You are not grieving wrong as long as you are staying connected to your heart. You are unique, and so is your pain. So, it makes sense that your ceremonies, your mile-markers on the map, may be something you have never seen or heard of. Follow your intuition and God's leading.

There is something very powerful about creating a physical and outward ritual to symbolize something that is happening internally. It does not magically take the pain away, but it does help your mind and spirit to have somewhere to focus the swirl of thoughts and feelings, and provides a way to move the grief out of your body and into reality. There is so much you cannot control, but being able to create a ritual helps give you a handle to hold onto, something that you *can* control. It pushes back against the sense of powerlessness that comes with trauma.

Rituals help us say goodbye to what was, and hello to what is. They are a boundary marker for us to measure a before and after. Looking back over my healing, I can see dozens of small ceremonies that were outward symbols of my inward reality. Two of these mile-markers stand out as especially important on my map: my "Ceremony of New Life," and my "Ceremony of Death."

Ceremony of New Life

It had been about a month since the affair had come to light, and my husband had made some significant steps towards me, with confession and accountability to others, access to his email and phone, and other assurances that I needed. He was answering all my questions, and I believed I saw remorse in him. He had moved back in and was staying in the basement until I was ready for us to share a room again. Each day was excruciating but I wanted to reconcile—not out of desperation, or trying to compete with the other woman, but because of my love for him. I felt strong and dignified and ready to take a meaningful step forward and welcome him back into covenant fully. So I invited him to make love to me. It was a beautiful moment, full of forgiveness, grace, and hope that seemed right and Spirit-led. I put on my white silk gown from our wedding night. I lit candles and with tears in my eyes, I anointed him with oil, declaring that he was clean, forgiven, and new. I offered my whole self to him. It was painful at moments, but it felt so holy. So hopeful.

I had no context for this kind of ceremony, but I created an experience to signify the start of a new, fresh marriage. It was a second wedding night. A new covenant. When I look back at that act of bravery and vulnerability and love, I am so proud of myself. I can say with full confidence that I did everything I could to keep my family together with my worth intact. I fell asleep with him beside me for the first time in months, and felt relief that we were heading in the right direction, together. I had such deep hope that we could rebuild.

But the next morning he could barely look at me. He told me he was going to look for apartments and moved all his things back into the basement. He couldn't do this with me.

I was gutted. My acceptance of him was rejected. My forgiveness of him was denied. My connection with him was severed. Again.

It may appear to some that this ceremony was wasted, or that this act was foolish. But I truly believe that *love is never wasted*. While I certainly experienced further exposure and pain because I opened up my heart again, I know that ritual had meaning that no rejection could take away. To this day, I have no regret over my Ceremony of New Life. I was my most honest, my most beautiful, my most brave self. It brought closure to my heart to know that I could go 'there', to that place of courage and risk and selflessness. He didn't have what it took to stay there, but I knew from then on that I did. This marked on my map that I was capable of reconciliation and full forgiveness.

For those whose story includes the resurrection of a marriage, and reconciliation, creating ceremonies with your spouse as you heal is a powerful way to bond and create closure together. Even though your marriage is mending, you are still walking through a grieving period. You may be mourning the loss of innocence, the trauma to your trust, or months or years of upheaval for your children . . . the list goes on. Just because you aren't divorced does not mean that you do not deserve the space and time you need to grieve, or the opportunity to tangibly express this process. Whether your rituals are done alone or together, these markers on your journey can be significant and healing. I know couples who burned separation papers after spending time in counseling and taking steps towards reconciliation, and many others who held vow renewal ceremonies to signify a fresh covenant. When these steps are unrushed and done honestly, they can represent a meaningful end to one chapter and a hope-filled start to a new one.

Ceremony of Death

My second ceremony was several months after our brief reconciliation. We were in the middle of the divorce, and while I had made concrete steps that had given me some closure, my heart needed something more. I journaled about it after our first legal mediation appointment.

That was awful.

We had a productive, but painful legal mediation today. It went 'well', but it was uncomfortable and devastating. It is not natural for a life, a home, a family to be divided. "Therefore what God has joined together, let no man tear asunder" (Matthew 19:6).

Yet asunder we are torn. Bits and pieces of identity and memories and promises are strewn haphazardly across the landscape of my life. Trying to survive the logistical surgery, the dissecting of my time, money, possessions, and children, is torture. God was gracious and gave me the poise and stamina to endure this phase of the process with my dignity intact. In reality it wasn't very dramatic. It was my lawyer and myself meeting with a nice older gentleman who went back and forth between rooms to negotiate an agreement. But you never imagine sitting in that chair, seeing a stranger scribble the details of your life, measuring up your worth in sums of assets and debts, reducing your sacred covenant to a math equation. This math is hard. And everyone loses.

It was pouring outside. Grey and dismal. I held it together, but the rain felt more authentic than the small talk and smiles.

After the meeting finished up, we walked to the elevator and the mediator and my lawyer jovially swapped stories about this judge and that attorney. This was just another normal day for them. Their lives consist of helping split up the spoils of what sin plunders from our lives. Honestly, bless them for it—us haggard travelers need some help sorting this crap out. But what a broken, hurting world.

The tears came once I was alone in my car. I started driving and quickly realized where my spirit was taking me.

"Oh. Oh, boy. Am I going to do this today? I guess I am."

Five and a half years ago my dreams were toppled with the loss of my first child. I grieved deeply and powerfully. It changed me, and that baby opened up channels in my heart that still allow perfect, golden light into my life. I memorialized that dear child near the river, burying a grain of rice to honor their short little life inside my womb. Today I revisited that sacred place to memorialize my deceased marriage.

By the time I arrived at the river, the sun was shining, and the sky was a piercing blue. I wept and wept and wept and wandered. I'm not crying nearly as much these days, and it felt so cleansing to empty my well of pain through those tears. I said goodbye, honored what was, and readied myself for what is to come.

The river was incredible. She moved me with her power. She was loud and fierce and determined. I was small and awestruck. There is so much in this world that is greater than ourselves. I couldn't help but worship and surrender to Jesus. I sang a song from my heart, and God was the only One who heard.

Jesus doesn't just save me from eternal damnation. He saves me in any moment in which I need saving. When I am in hell, He brings heaven. He is beautiful, swift, merciful, and radically more creative than I ever dared dream. He is crafting something stunning from my shattered heart, I can feel it.

Today was a burial. It was somber and painful. It was beautiful and important. Yet even as I grieved and ached, I heard the whispered promise of spring in the wind. The vibrant green in the moss and the grass hinted that something different is coming. A resurrection, a rebirth, a fresh start. In Christ, I am a new creation: Old things have passed away; behold, all things are being made new.

This burial was another mile-marker in my healing. It acknowledged outwardly to me that my marriage was dead. I considered the divorce paperwork to be the death certificate, but just as in grieving a dead loved one, filling out forms did not feel like an adequate way to say goodbye. I needed to go to a special place, say the words out loud, and then leave. In the middle of a season that had so much nebulous and undefined transition, it felt good to do something that had a beginning and end.

There were numerous other rituals that helped me move the weight of the emotion I was carrying out of my body. The night I found my husband with his mistress, I threw all of our framed wedding photos on the sidewalk outside of our home, smashing the glass to pieces. It symbolized outwardly what had happened in my heart. This was not a pre-planned, intentional ritual. It was a visceral reaction that felt very primal. But looking back, I can see that my body and brain needed a physical expression of the intensity I was holding within myself.

The shirt he was wearing the night I caught him in the affair was seared into my brain. I was so triggered every time I saw him wearing it. Thankfully I talked him into giving it to me, and one night after I dropped off our children at his apartment, I was driving downtown and I threw it out the window. It was a nice shirt, and I hoped that one of the homeless men in the area would find it and put it to good use. I don't recommend littering like that, but I would have gladly paid a ticket for that ritual. It was a relief to not have that trigger in my world anymore.

One ritual (which many of the women I've coached have also found helpful) is writing down the things I am struggling to release control over on a piece of paper. It could be the name of a person, a re-occurring worry, or a memory I want to let go of. I then take the paper, hold it over a jar, and light it on fire. In order for me to not get burned, I have to let go. The physical act of letting go symbolizes the internal letting go. The jar full of ash is a reminder to me that I have released these things to the Lord, and I cannot take them back.

The list goes on, but you can see that there is no prescription to what kind of rituals can bring closure. Things that may feel insignificant to someone else may be a mile-marker on your map that helps you turn a corner. You have full permission to create a moment that helps you express your emotion in a tangible way. Without closure, the loose ends of grief can make you feel tossed around with nothing to hold onto. Closing the loop and tying things together one thread at a time is the wearying work of grief. It can feel overwhelming to even know how to start, but bit by bit, day by day, ritual by ritual, you will begin to see the jumbled, fraying mess come back together, taking shape. As you put markers on your map, you will begin to see how far you have come.

PRAYER

God, only You can understand the depth of my grief. There are not words to describe it. Thank You for knowing me and my pain and staying close to me in it. Please help me to walk through it and not avoid or bury it. As I do the hard work of moving towards acceptance, thank You for Your patience and grace over me. Hold me while I feel the intensity of my emotions. Give me wisdom on how to create closure and courage to walk with You through this.

APPLICATION

1. Practice saying "Hello" to an emotion you are experiencing. What does it want to tell you about why it is there?

2. Are there layers of your grief that feel too 'wild' for you? If you have fears about letting it out, list what those may be. Explore what it might feel like to give yourself permission to be free to release it.

3. What is one point of pain that you feel a lack of closure about? Ask God to give you insight into creating a ritual around this pain-point. Feel free to ask for ideas from safe support people in your life. Once you have collated your thoughts, identify one ritual that you can schedule this week.

I am but a breath
You, eternal wind
My heart is caged in my chest
Yours, wild beyond the world

Yet you bless my brevity
Caress my small existence
With the tender joy
Of a doting Parent

My life is not a test,
But a beautiful unfurling—
Agony when resisted
Bliss when surrendered

You romance me—
Evening light in the curtains
The heavy comfort of a quilt
A child's small hand on my arm

Creative Creator,
You make everything I love
And set me loose on your Earth
To choose freedom or fear

Will my life be a gasp?
Or a soft, gentle sigh
Wrapped in peace and warm trust
Blown to the edge of another's pain

Holy power in feeble hands
Holy music on unclean lips
Holy love in my fragile heart—
You are not afraid to share

May my life breath
Be the sweet exhale
Of Good News—
Wild Wind, sweeping us Home

12

HEALING

BEING HELD BY JESUS

I had given my husband my whole heart, and when he rejected it, tossing it aside on the ground, I realized that I had a choice to pick it back up or leave it there. Who else would care for it if not me? I prayed and hoped and longed for him to want it back, to start afresh, to help me heal it. But when he chose to forsake it forever, I was determined to care for it well. I lost him. I lost us. But I did not lose myself.

Healing is not measured by the survival of your marriage, or your ability to influence the actions of your spouse. Healing is measured by walking through this trial without losing your own heart. You may not get to choose whether or not you lose his heart, but you do get to choose to keep yours.

I have seen so many women trade their spirit for a counterfeit, one that is defined by rejection or revenge. Do not be fooled by the allure of bitterness. Do not believe the lie that you are safer if you shut down. Hold onto your heart. I know it hurts, and you may want to bury it. But the pain is a sign of life. Your heart aches because it is alive. The bravest thing you can do is to keep it soft. Keep it open. Not necessarily to your husband—if he is not safe, boundaries are needed for both of your sakes. But keep your heart open to yourself, and to Jesus.

RELEASING YOUR GRIP

There is an inner knowing only you have about whether or not you are open to the Lord. Be honest with yourself. It is normal, and understandable to feel the need to close yourself off to any and all connection because you have been wounded so acutely. But you can trust Jesus. He really is the only way to your healing, and He longs to hold and comfort you.

As I said before, Jesus heals everything we allow Him to touch. Sometimes we hold back from Him or hold on to the pain because of muscle memory. Maybe we have carried this hurt for so long, through so many dark nights, that we do not know how to pry our fingers from it. Or perhaps there is a strange comfort in such a familiar thing, and though it cuts us to hold it, we know what to expect. It feels like control, even as we bleed. Sometimes we identify so much with the pain that we don't know who we will be without it—without the sympathy, the attention, the connection it brings us. What if we don't want to lose that?

Or maybe, if we get really honest, the deep down, gritty kind of honest, we just don't trust Him enough. We want the explanation, the justification, the answer to the 'why' first. But friend, doesn't it get heavy to carry this pain alone?

Look at Him. Look at His hands. These are the kind of hands we can trust. Scarred by love, big enough to hold the whole world, gentle and strong. Look again, in His eyes. He cares for you. Do you see it? These eyes have seen it all, cried an ocean of tears, and gazed into a future your mind cannot contain. It takes courage to release your grip and allow Him to touch the pain. You've been hurt when you trusted before. I understand. But His touch healed my heart more than any self-help strategy, counseling session, length of time, or any other thing.

In those early days as I lay in bed, alone, I would be reminded of the loss of physical connection with my husband. I ached to be held. I would often reach out and touch where my husband's body used to lay next to me. Longing and disgust would fill me, simultaneously. How could I miss the dagger that had pierced my heart? How could I want to be touched by the hands that had moved over another woman's body? How is it possible those same hands were the ones our children fell into during their first steps? Those hands held my hair during bouts of stomach flu and pregnancy nausea. They cooked my favorite meals, clapped and cheered at my performances and races; they wiped my tears. I held those hands through years of memories, and they had felt like home. Now the thought of them sent chills of dread through me.

Yet I knew I was made for connection, for closeness. My love language had always been physical touch, even from childhood. When my mom scratched my back, or my daddy wrapped me up in a long bear hug, it made me feel secure and loved. I remember one night, as tears soaked into my pillow, asking Jesus to hold me. I was desperate and lonely and broken. I believed He was with me, but I wanted to *feel Him*.

So, I asked to be held.

Suddenly, I was aware of His love wrapping me up, holding me close, warming my skin. It was beyond physical. My heart was being held by God. Every night after that I met Him there and let Him hold me, allowing His love to wash over me while I just cried in His arms. My spirit was so open to His, and I found an intimacy there that I had never known. The God of the universe held me. I sensed His tenderness towards me as night after night I turned my affection toward Him, reaching out in my deepest pain and loneliness, and He responded. God's presence became more real to me in the hurt than I had ever known before.

If we seek Him on our darkest nights, we will find Him, and our hearts will echo the words of the psalmist, David:

> *"I lie awake thinking of you, meditating on you through the night.*

Because you are my helper, I sing for joy in the shadow of your wings. I cling to you; your strong right hand holds me securely."

Psalm 63:6-8

David wrote these kinds of poem-songs while he was still hurting and being pressed by evil. He was running for his life and hiding in the wilderness, yet as he clung to God, he understood he was held securely, regardless of what his circumstances looked like. Those same strong, safe, scarred hands are here to hold you.

MOVING FORWARD, LEANING IN

As I began to heal, held in God's hands, I still felt as though I was on a roller-coaster. The twists and turns, the sharp descents that left my stomach in my throat continued to thrash me around. But as time passed, I found that the triggers happened less frequently. It still hurt just as badly, but not as often. Writing out my thoughts and feelings helped ground me. Here's an excerpt from my journal:

I'm hurting tonight.

I don't know how to do this. How to be strong and firm without fueling anger and bitterness. How to be soft and forgiving without being crushed. My soul is sore and tired. Some days I feel so completely at the end of my rope that I'm certain I cannot hold it together one more second.

Then the clock ticks.

I'm somehow still here. Surrendering to the process. Trusting God is holding and guiding me. Giving myself margins to be a total wreck so that I can wipe off the tears and the grime and the lies and keep trekking on.

This beast is a moving target. It's a strange and unnatural loss. There is no final punctuation. It's not a full death, because I still see him. He's alive, but not mine. Habits die hard, mind games await, heart strings are plucked, new normals need establishing. The grief is stirred not just by memory, but by new wounds. It is a relentless deluge of "not the way it's meant to be." And yet...

HEALING

It is incredible how grief sways and wells and subsides. She is an unpredictable dancer. Yet somehow the way she moves is so correct. So in sync with the rhythm inside me. So wise. I'm learning to yield.

So, if right now I feel alive, refreshed, empowered and hopeful? Great—lean in. And if now I feel ragged, violated, exposed, and afraid? Okay—lean in. Just show up and trust the journey. No matter what I feel, I am not alone. God is here. Lean in. It's when people resist or hide that the healing halts. And that's okay too—maybe we need a break from healing sometimes. It's hard work.

But I'm too tired to resist. And I'm too transparent to hide. I'm going deep and fast. Healing is happening, and it's kicking my butt.

I am mourning and celebrating. Part of me is dying and part of me is being born. I am weeping and somehow the tears act as lenses, giving clarity and sharp distinction to all that is True. I am devastated and liberated. Broken and better than ever. Stripped bare and clothed in mercy and goodness. I am saying Goodbye and Hello.

This is a matchless time of riches for me. I'm already able to say that I'm right where I'm meant to be. I feel God so near, and this brokenness has opened me up to Him. That is priceless, and I am grateful. But suffering is SO HARD! It is a grace that these seasons are intermittent, treasure troves that they are. It is like staring at the sun. It's a source of great light, but we aren't meant to look for long.

So, tonight is a lull, a lag, a valley. The sword pierces the side. But the sun will rise in the morning. Tomorrow is a new day. I am doing the hard work and someday grief will give way to wholeness.

"Lord haste the day where my faith shall be sight."

Looking back on that season, I have such tenderness towards that version of myself, pushing through the pain towards the light. I can honestly say that He has made my faith sight, as I walk in deep healing and freedom in this season of my life. There is not one wound that Jesus hasn't touched and healed. What was meant to destroy me brought me more life than I even had before.

As you walk forward into healing, don't be discouraged by fresh waves of grief, anger, or pain. You are still moving forward! There is no shame in accepting the emotions that come. It doesn't mean you are losing ground; it is just another opportunity for you to lean into. Accepting the waves, letting them do their work, and knowing that they are bringing progress can help us cope with the pain and give us hope.

I also want to encourage you that it is possible to feel more than one thing at once. Sometimes it can feel confusing or disingenuous to have a truly great day, or a moment of excitement or joy in the middle of a huge trial. But your heart was created to hold more than one emotion at a time. You can experience pain and peace, weakness and strength, heartache and hope together. The author of Hebrews tells us that Jesus endured the suffering and pain of the cross "for the joy set before Him" (Hebrews 12:2). He held suffering and joy together in a beautiful tension, and we can too.

GOING DEEPER

The affair caused every insecurity I had lived out since childhood to resurface. As I wrestled with the lies the enemy flung at me, it seemed like the affair proved my inmost doubts. I had always been afraid I was unlovable, and this made that fear come to life. Every rejection and embarrassment from my whole life seemed to pile up into one moment, and I felt buried by it. The enemy was trying to leverage every awkward middle school locker-room memory, every whispered word and laugh about me on the school bus, every time I was passed over, misunderstood, and rejected. It was not enough for the enemy to destroy my marriage; He wanted to destroy me too.

What the enemy did not anticipate, however, was that I would take every hurt to God. Old questions about my worth and identity were answered in fresh love by my Jesus. Slowly, surely, I began to feel a power and a strength rise up in me in response to these attacks. As I took every question to Jesus about who I really was, He answered. The truth began to fill my heart and God's nearness and goodness emboldened me. As I recovered my footing in life, I walked with more assurance and confidence than before the attack of the affair. The plan to destroy me had backfired. I knew who I was, what I could endure, and Who held me together.

You may also find that the wound of the affair is triggering other pain from your past. It is almost as though there is a deep place inside us where the pain is held, and when something reaches down to that place, it jostles all the other memories of wounds that have lived there. It can feel unfair to have to deal with issues from your childhood, or family members, or past relationships. But there is a gift in the exposure because it can allow the light of more healing to enter in.

I have walked with countless women who, while healing from the affair, have had the courage and perseverance to address lies they believed about themselves, reaching back into their early childhood or adolescence. It is almost as if being forced into the gaping wounds of trauma enables us to access parts of our heart that we may have buried, forgotten, or shielded, even if we weren't aware of it. This access can result in more wholeheartedness, more self-awareness than we have ever had before. It is a costly time, but the reward is rich for those who do the digging.

I encourage you to find someone safe, such as a trusted friend, counselor, or pastor, who can dig with you and give you the perspective and support you need. Your biggest wounds have come from relationship, so your biggest healing will come from relationship. Nothing combats rejection like acceptance, nothing destroys insecurity like affirmation, and nothing dismantles lies like the truth. Even though the relationship may be a different type—perhaps a friend instead of your spouse—relational healing can still touch those deepest parts of your heart.

HEALING WELL

It is not enough to just let time take away the edge. We want to heal *well*. A bone needs to be aligned to heal well and not cause future pain and limitation. Rather than just letting a broken leg be left alone, which may feel better in the moment, but will no doubt lead to a life-long limp and disfigurement, we need to make sure we put things in place, even if it hurts.

The heart is the same. God's ways are like a brace, holding us in place while we mend. Obedience to God's Word is wisdom in healing. Trust Him! Any limit He puts on us is for our own safety. Pain does not give us an excuse to disobey His voice. In fact, obedience is never more important than when we are broken. I am not saying it is easy. There was a part of me during my healing that wanted to just go wild. There was a temptation to loosen and lower my standards because I was hurt. Deep inside, I knew that thrashing around in sin was only going to hurt me more and increase my injury. I needed to be held in place by righteousness to heal well.

It is normal to be tempted to numb your pain. Binging Netflix, food, alcohol, etc. may entice you to just get a break, but be careful to not walk outside of where God is calling you to walk. While most things are healthy in moderation, there is a real temptation to move into excess when you are in pain. God will show you where the line is for you—it is not always the same for every person. Guard your heart, mind and body during this vulnerable time.

It is also tempting to walk straight into sin when you've been violated like this. It's normal to think about what it would feel like to retaliate, and just go find some other man to have sex with. After all, you've been hurt and deserve some, right? Wrong. You will regret that, sister. Do not accept anything less than covenant love. You do not need to be ashamed if you find yourself tempted in this way—Jesus was tempted (e.g., Matthew 4:1-11, Hebrews 4:15). But do not believe for one moment that sexual sin will fix the damage made by sexual sin. One of the most useful definitions of sin that I have found is from Ignatius of Loyola who said sin is "an unwillingness to trust that what God wants for me is only my deepest happiness." In order to find the healing we desire, we must trust that God wants what is best for us, and has the right to define what that is, and what it is not. Of course, if you have made mistakes and sinned during your recovery time, there is always hope and healing for you! Simply turn to Jesus, acknowledge your lack, and receive His forgiveness. He is faithful to forgive and guide you back into healing.

To come back to the analogy of the broken bone, there is some additional work that must be done to rebuild strength as the healing progresses. Anyone who has done physical therapy knows that this work is *not pleasant*. It causes pain to prevent long term damage. There is often stretching and a process of learning to bear weight again. In the same way, asking ourselves hard questions and bearing the weight of any personal responsibility helps us heal well.

Again, I want to be crystal clear—you bear no responsibility for your husband's choice to engage in an affair. However, it is important as we heal to ask what actions we have made that have contributed to our own suffering. For me, it meant that following our divorce, I had to ask myself questions like: *Why do I continue to seek validation from someone I no longer trust? Why am I breaking my own boundaries of communication? If I have released him from being my husband, why am I still expecting him to act like he is and then getting disappointed when he is not?* As I wrestled with these questions, my healing muscles stretched and strengthened, even as it hurt.

It is important to realize that you can heal well and still bear scars. Even Jesus, in His perfected, resurrection body, has scars that tell His story. There is something beautiful and profound about that. God Himself wears scars. So do not be ashamed of yours. There is no going back to our original form. For me, the love and loss and healing were worth the marks, and I do not hide them. There is power in the testimony of what we have survived.

LAYERS OF HEALING

Healing will take time. While the majority of my healing happened within the first year after the affair, there were layers that took years to be uncovered. It is actually a grace and mercy that we do not endure all the pain all at once! It can be discouraging to feel like you are not 'done', but part of the healing process really is allowing the time that is needed.

I recently watched a documentary about sea life and learned that when a mother Orca whale loses her young, she will stay with the dead body for up to weeks at a time. It moved me to tears. If even animals honor their loss with time, how much more can we give ourselves permission to allow time to process and cope with our grief? There is no strict timeline; your healing journey will be as unique as you are. Be gentle with yourself.

Do not be surprised when you feel like you have made a lot of progress and then—Bam!—you feel hit with another surge of pain or anger that stirs you up again. You are not doing anything wrong to cause this! It is a normal part of the journey. Remind yourself that you know how to do this. You have built healing muscles. You have strategies that have worked well before. Use them again, and you will likely find that you can enter into peace and stability with more speed and confidence than you could at the start.

One thing that has been helpful for me is to think of healing as something that I have not obtained and can therefore lose. Instead, healing, like forgiveness, is a place in which I can live. I live *inside* healing, hidden in Christ. So, it is not so much something I 'have' or have 'done'. If I cannot say I am healed, I can at least say that I am living in healing. Healing is a place. And healing is a Person. When I lose my way, I can come back to that place, with Jesus. *In Him.* I do not have to fight for healing, strive for it, earn it. I get to rest in it, accept it, and soak it in.

While I still occasionally struggle with frustration about not 'being done', I find such peace and gratitude in looking at how far I have come. I am now able to revisit all of the memories surrounding the affair with little to no pain resurfacing. Similar to childbirth, I remember the pain and have compassion for myself as I recall the intensity, but I no longer experience the pain in the present moment. I can share my story with the women who I coach through their own pain, without feeling drained or triggered. Because of the healing God has walked me through, my story is now a source of strength and hope for me to draw from.

God wants to turn your story from a tragedy to a testimony as well. As you invite Him in to re-write any part of you that needs His touch, you will be amazed at how He transforms your brokenness into beauty.

PRAYER

God, I want to heal. I long to live inside of Your healing that You purchased for me with Your own blood. Please help me stay close to You. I cannot heal right on my own. I give You my wounded heart and ask You to touch it. Guide me and help me obey You. As I walk through each layer of hurt, help me to lean in and trust You to help me not only survive this, but to heal well. Give me strength to press into the pain when I need to, and wisdom to know when I need a break. Thank You for holding me close and for covering me with Your endless love.

APPLICATION

1. How have you experienced God in a new or deeper way in this season?

2. How does the idea of being *inside* healing feel different than *finishing* healing?

3. What part of your pain might you need to lean into, in order to bring another layer of healing?

Promises kept.
Answers tucked into
Small spaces
Beauty blooming slow

It is never
All at once.
One spirit cannot
Finish the full work

Single grains of sand
Collect, forming the coast
Of my stormy soul—
A new home

Each addition
Breaks my heart open
Heals a piece
Changes the landscape

God-given manna
Word, touch, look
Honey on my tongue
Lord, let me savor

Light streams down
Waves calm
Caress the shore
Once wrecked by their power

I am so little
And so much
So fearfully vast
And so simple

You are the same
A world of stories
A sea of memories
A universe of wonder

Passing handfuls of sand
From my shore to yours
Transformed eternal
Gifts between and within

You are a surprise
A passing breeze
Shifting the earth
Refreshing my hope

EPILOGUE

As I reflect on my life over the past eight-and-a-half years since my world shattered, I am in awe. God has done such a profound healing in my heart and life.

I remember shortly after I had found out about the affair, I was walking along the river near my old home with a new-found friend. A few years prior, her husband had left her for another woman while she was pregnant with their third child. When I had heard about her story I was horrified and grieved for her. Now it was my turn to live the nightmare. I was gutted, my heart was defeated, and I was barely hanging on. But seeing the compassion and life in her eyes, hearing the steadiness and peace in her voice, shifted something inside me. *This will be you, someday. You will walk alongside other women, speaking the same hope and truth over them. You will be whole.*

I believed her healing was real. I knew mine was coming.

The seed of this book was planted in those early days, and I have carried it in my heart all these years. When God whispered that it was time, I was ready. How wonderful of Him to wait until the pain had subsided enough for me to wade back into the deep for hours every week, writing and remembering and writing some more. He knew my scars were thick enough for me to remember without injury. And how wise of Him to not wait any longer, or the memories may have become so thin and blurry that they would be out of my reach. Truly, He makes all things beautiful in His time.

It may seem hard to believe, but I really am so grateful that God trusted me with this brokenness. Even in the midst of my deepest pain, I had a sense that I was created for this. That my heart was built to carry the weight of the hurt *and* the healing. Even though I railed against the loss and ached for a different story, I have a deep knowing that God has purposed to waste *nothing* in my life. And now, on the other side of the abyss, I would not have it any other way.

Of course, I still mourn for my children and their loss. I know the darkness still seeks to exact more pain from them, and from me as the years go on. And I know God did not design the sin and torment that broke the marriage. Yet, He uses it. To bless me. To bless the women I coach and counsel. And I pray, to bless *you*.

While my story is still being written as my life unfolds, I can honestly say the Lord has restored the years that the locust had eaten. I found my healing in Jesus and still do. The work He did in my heart in that first year especially, was breathtaking. The strength and grace I found was nothing short of a miracle.

In time, God led me to meet my best friend, Severin, who carries scars matching mine. I could write a whole other book about the journey of opening one's heart to love again after healing from such a deep wound, but suffice it to say, God answered both of our prayers. We are both still in awe of the redemption God has worked in our relationship and the lives of our children as we became a family. I did not know that love could be so true and steady. I have never felt more known, more free, more protected, and more whole than I have in this marriage. Remarriage and blending a family have carried unique challenges, but this beautiful life we have built together is more than I could have hoped for. Even among juggling parenting plans and co-parenting and lost time with our children, our cups overflow with goodness.

My life has reflected the story of my namesake in the Bible, Ruth the Moabite. Just as Ruth mourned the loss of one husband and of a life she loved, and was led into frightening unknowns, the

God she chose to follow led her with unending faithfulness. He restored her and secured her, blessed her in a second marriage, and rewarded her faithfulness with the gift of being grafted into the line of David. Her lineage led to Jesus, and her obedience despite the tragedies she faced, allowed her to be a part of the greatest story ever told. He has led me with the same faithfulness, and my prayer is that my life and my obedience would also put the faithfulness and goodness of God on full display and lead people to Jesus. *He* is the hero of my story.

APPENDIX

FORGIVING YOUR HUSBAND

Pray and ask God to help you prepare your heart for forgiveness.

Ask God to show you how He sees your husband. What is He showing you?

Take some time to write out an inventory of what you need to forgive your husband for. The list may be long.

Ask the Lord to give you strength to forgive each item. Speak out the forgiveness, "Jesus, I forgive _____ for _____."

If you become too overwhelmed to finish the list, take your time. Address one item on the list each time you come to pray.

If you are reconciling, it will be important for you to share this list with your husband. If you are not reconciling, consider sharing this list with a pastor or trusted friend for additional closure.

If you are not reconciling, I recommend a prayer to break all soul ties with your husband. "Father, as I forgive _____, I break every soul tie that was created during our covenant. I release them from my judgment into Your hands, and I sever the heart connection that was between us."

FORGIVING THE OTHER WOMAN

Pray and ask God to help you prepare your heart for forgiveness.

Ask Him to show you how He sees this woman. What is He showing you?

Take a moment to pray for her. Even if your prayer is forced, or short, God will bless your effort. As you heal, return to praying for her when you feel anger rising against her.

When you are ready, write out your forgiveness to this woman, using her name.

If you have the opportunity and the courage to read this to her in person, or mail her this message, I encourage you to do so. It may take some time to be able to take that step. Pray and ask God for wisdom about the timing and delivery. If you are unable to do that, it may be very healing to have a trusted friend stand in for her.

RECOMMENDED RESOURCES

1. *Divorce and Remarriage in the Church*, by David Instone-Brewer (InterVarsity Press, 2003).

2. *How to Help Your Spouse Heal from Your Affair: A Compact Manual for the Unfaithful,* by Linda J. MacDonald (Healing Counsel Press, 2010).

3. *The Covenants* by Kevin J. Conner and Ken Malmin (City Bible Publishing, 1983).

4. *What to Do When He Says, I Don't Love You Anymore: An Action Plan to Regain Confidence, Power and Control,* by David Clarke (Thomas Nelson, 2002).

ACKNOWLEDGMENTS

To the team of professionals who made this book happen:

Anya McKee and the team at Torn Curtain Publishing – Thank you for following the call of God on your life! Authors across the world are being equipped and released because of your courage and gifting. Thank you for mentoring and gently guiding this book into production. I felt safe, empowered and resourced through every step. A thousand thanks would not suffice!

Aimée Walker – I am so grateful for the God connection across the Pacific! Thank you for your wisdom, advice and encouragement when this book was in seed form. You are a mouthpiece of God.

Sarah Mejia – Your prophetic artistry has transposed my writing and the vision of this book into visual beauty. Your creativity is intuitive, elegant and powerful. Thank you for making everything you touch more lovely.

Mike Monroe – Thank you for energizing me with such dense and powerful marketing insight. Your gifts to me will help this book reach exponentially more women than I could have done on my own.

To my dear friends and church family:

Amy Mundo – Thank you for the writing dates, your encouragement and belief in me as a writer, and the beautiful deposit you made into this book. I am forever grateful to you, friend!

Morgan Stigall – Your pioneering courage impacts me as a friend, minister and writer. Thank you for your practical encouragement in the early manuscript days and for showing me that writing a book while raising kids and working is doable!

Jasmine Momeni – My fire sister. Going deep into the flames with you during the writing of this book gave the spark it needed to come to life. We did this together, and I have never been so honored to witness a life poured out for Jesus.

Crystal Kreager – Your discernment and wisdom have given me such strength. Working with you has been a pure joy. Your grit and boss lady vibes have rubbed off on me and given me new levels of courage and determination. You're kind of a big deal.

Lindsey Ecklund – Your hugs have held me together for years, and I am so honored to do life with you. Thank you for always seeing me, loving me, and believing in me. You are a treasure.

Joel Ecklund – Your prophetic presence and faithful friendship are such gifts to me, brother! Thanks for being my theology friend and for digging deep wells of worship with me.

Jeff Ecklund – Your covering and the way you have called out the gifts in me means more than I could ever say. I am so proud to call you my pastor, and it is an honor to serve Jesus' Bride with you.

Susie Ingold – God has spoiled me with you! Your rich love has brought me encouragement, direction, strength and clarity. I love being in His presence with you and ministering to His daughters together. Thank you for believing in me so fiercely. Let the Lion roar!

Kristen Carter – From the births of my babies, to the death of my first marriage, to the rebirth of my broken heart, you have been close, steady, wise and brave. You called out strength and beauty in me during my most vulnerable moments, and I could never express how grateful I am for your life-changing friendship.

To my family:

Franny – I love the passion and love in your sweet heart. Thank you for planning the best experiences and for modeling consistent adventure!

Toby – Your quiet strength and deep love are such a gift. Thank you for the intention and attention you give my children, Uncle Bobo.

Tina – You have seen it all. Your goodness and wisdom have anchored and upheld me through every storm. Thank you for being my person for decades.

Billy – Your fierce protection and love has been more healing than you will ever know, my brother. You are my favorite debate partner, and I am glad teenage me decided to like you after all.

Bekah – You ask the greatest questions, and I love the deep deposit of wisdom inside you. Thank you for carrying peace and light into every room.

Reed – Thank you for your sharp insight and brave example. You inspire and motivate me to take up more space and go hard after the call on my life.

Mom – You held me so close during my fire that you got burned. Thank you for your enduring love, wisdom, and for nurturing the deepest, hidden, best parts of my heart. I want to be like you when I grow up.

Dad – Making you proud is my favorite thing. Thank you for pouring out your love and delight over my life. You have always pointed me to Jesus and modeled the Father's love as clearly as you can. I'm grateful to be your girl.

My children – The four of you are the lights of my life, and proof of God's goodness. Conner, your gentle and wise soul won me over from the start. Thank you for leading your siblings so well. Landon, your compassion and brilliant mind are such gifts to this world and our family. Keep thinking and feeling deeply. Keller, your tenderness and loyalty make you such an incredible friend and son. You melt me. Thea, you are glitter and spice, and you complete our family. You shine bright, and we all adore you!

Severin – Words cannot come close to describing my love and gratitude for who you are. You are the answer to the deepest cries and prayers of my heart. Your steady, unshakable, uncomplicated love has changed me, wooing me into the best version of myself. Thank you for all of the little and big things you have sacrificed to lift me up. You cover, protect and provide for me in a way that never limits me. I am amazed by you.

To my Creator God, the One in the fire with me:

Father, You guarded me from the flames with Your mighty hand and delivered me up onto high ground. Jesus, You wept and bled with me and healed me by Your stripes. Spirit, You breathed new life and power into me and filled me with Your fire to push back darkness. To You I offer my everything. You are worthy of it all.

For additional free resources from Ruth, please visit:

www.RuthEricksonResource.com

www.ingramcontent.com/pod-product-compliance
Lightning Source LLC
Chambersburg PA
CBHW020319010526
44107CB00054B/1905